Side

Hustle

Investing

for

Beginners

How to Turn Your Passion into a
Profitable Investment

Gilbert Predmore

Table of Contents

Chapter 3: Common Side Hustle Investing Mistakes to Avoid

Chapter 4: Case Studies of Successful Side Hustle Investors

Author's Preface

I've always had a love for online business. I remember when I was just a kid, I would spend hours on the internet, reading websites and trying to figure out how they worked. I was fascinated by the idea of being able to make something and share it with the world, and I dreamed of one day having my own famous online business.

As I grew older, I started to learn more about investments. I learned that trading could be a great way to grow my wealth and achieve my financial goals. But I also understood that buying could be dangerous, and I didn't want to put all my eggs in one box.

That's when I had the thought of joining my two passions: online business and investments. I learned that I could use my knowledge of online business to build side hustles that would make cash for me. And then I could invest that salary to grow my wealth even faster.

I started small, with just a few simple side hustles. But over time, my side hustles grew and became more valuable. And as my side hustles grew, so did my stock account.

Today, I'm living my dream. I have a great online business, and I'm able to spend my earnings to grow my wealth even faster. I'm financially independent, and I have the freedom to do whatever I want.

I wrote this book to help other people achieve their cash goals. I want to teach you how to start and grow side hustles, and how to spend your earnings carefully. I want to show you that it is possible to achieve financial freedom, even if you don't have a lot of money to start with.

In this book, you will learn:
- How to find and start successful side hustles
- How to grow your side hustles and scale your income
- How to invest your side hustle earnings wisely
- How to build a varied investment portfolio
- How to achieve financial freedom

I know personally what it's like to be broke and trying to make ends meet. I also know what it's like to achieve financial independence and have the freedom to do whatever I want.

I think that everyone deserves to have financial freedom. That's why I'm writing this book to teach people how to start and grow side hustles, and how to spend their earnings carefully.

I hope that this book will help you to achieve your financial goals and live your best life.

Introduction

What is side hustle investing?

Side hustle investing is the practice of using the earnings from a side hustle to invest in assets that have the potential to generate income or grow in value over time. This can be a great way to boost your savings, reach your financial goals faster, and build wealth.

Why side hustle investing is a good idea for beginners

Side work investing is a great way for newbies to learn about investing and start building their wealth. It helps you to invest with a smaller amount of money and take on less risk than if you were to invest full-time.

Here are some of the perks of side hustle trading for beginners:
- It's a low-risk way to learn about business.

When you're first starting out, it's important to learn about different business items and methods before you put a lot of money into them. Side hustle investing allows you to try with different businesses and see what works best for you without losing your entire financial future.

- It can help you build your financial discipline. Side work investing requires you to be careful with your money and stick to your investment plan. This is a useful skill to learn, as it will help you achieve over the long run.

- It can help you reach your cash goals faster. Investing in your side hustle can help you reach your financial goals faster, such as saving for a down payment on a house or retirement. Even if you can only spend a small amount each month, it will add up over time.

How to choose a side hustle to invest in

When picking a side hustle to invest in, it's important to consider several factors to ensure it fits with your skills, hobbies, and financial goals. Here are some key things to keep in mind:

1. Identify Your Skills and Interests:

Consider what you are good at and what you love doing. Your side job should match with your skills and hobbies, making it more rewarding and sustainable in the long run.

2. Market study:
Conduct thorough study to discover profitable and in-demand side job ideas. Analyze industry trends, competition, and possible customer groups. This will help you choose an area with growth prospects.

3. Assess Time Commitment:
Evaluate how much time you can realistically commit to your side job. Some projects take more time and effort than others, so choose one that fits your plan and lifestyle.

4. Financial Investment:
Determine how much money you are willing to spend initially. Some side hustles require significant upfront investment, while others can be started with limited funds. Consider your price limits and choose accordingly.

5. Evaluate Risk Tolerance:

All purchases come with a certain amount of risk. Assess your risk tolerance and choose a side job that fits with your comfort level. Diversifying your finances can also help spread the risk.

6. Networking and Support:
Connect with people who are already successful in your chosen area. Networking can provide useful insights and support, helping you overcome obstacles and learn from others' experiences.

7. Legal and Regulatory Compliance:
Understand the legal and regulatory standards connected with your chosen side job. Ensure that you meet with all necessary licenses, permits, and tax responsibilities to avoid legal problems later on.

8. Test the Waters:
Consider starting your side job on a small scale originally to test its potential. This allows you to measure the market reaction and make necessary changes before fully committing your time and resources.

9. Long-Term Viability:

Think about the long-term possibilities of your side job. Is it a trend that might fade away, or does it have the possibility for continued growth? Choose a business with a safe future for long financial benefits.

10. Passion and Perseverance:

Lastly, be excited about your chosen side job and be prepared to put in consistent effort. Perseverance is key to beating obstacles and finding success in any business venture.

By considering these factors, you can make a well-informed choice when picking a side job to invest in, improving your chances of financial success and personal happiness.

How to get started with side hustle investing

Embarking on the path of side hustle investing is akin to falling into the pages of a fascinating book, full with endless opportunities and rewarding experiences. Just like a reader dives into a book, you can engage yourself in the world of business and financial growth.

First and foremost, treat your business like a well-researched book. Begin by reading widely about various side job ideas, discovering different types of businesses, and knowing the market trends. Just as a reader immerses themselves in the story, allow yourself to dive deep into the details of possible investments. Learn from the stories of great businesses, getting lessons from their successes and challenges.

As you would choose a book that fits with your interests, pick a side job that connects with your skills and hobbies. Your financial trip, much like reading, should be a pleasant and interesting experience. Consider your skills, hobbies, and the things that truly excite you. This human link will not only keep you inspired but also improve your chances of success.

Just like a reader talks about their favorite books with fellow lovers, engaging in chats with experienced businesses and teachers. Seek help from those who have walked the same path before you. Books can be a source of inspiration; similarly, teachers can provide useful advice and support, helping you manage the complicated parts of your business story.

Remember, every great book takes time and commitment to read, understand, and enjoy fully. Similarly, your side hustle investment requires patience, perseverance, and regular effort. Embrace the learning curve, enjoy the difficulties, and celebrate your successes, no matter how small they may seem. With every part you read, and every step you take in your side hustle journey, you are writing your own story of success.

So, dear reader-turned-entrepreneur, approach your side job investment with the excitement of a reader discovering a new literature world. With the right attitude, knowledge, and desire, you're bound to create a story of financial growth and personal satisfaction that matches the most engaging of stories. Happy reading and buying!

Chapter 1

Low-Cost Side Hustle Investment Strategies

Micro Investing

Micro-investing is a modern method of trading where people can put small amounts of money into financial tools such as stocks, exchange-traded funds (ETFs), or other assets. This democratization of investing opens doors for individuals who might have found standard investment methods difficult or financially out of reach.

Micro-investing sites usually offer partial shares, allowing buyers to buy a piece of a share rather than a whole share. This method makes it easier for newbies to spread their investments across multiple assets, even with limited funds. By spending small amounts regularly, individuals can possibly grow their wealth over time, benefit from compound interest, and join in the financial markets without a sizable upfront investment.

Benefits for newbies include low entry hurdles, cost, diversity, training tools, automation and ease, and no need for stock picking. Traditional trading usually means getting whole shares, which can be expensive for high-value stocks. Micro-investing platforms often have lower fees and charges compared to traditional trading accounts, making it cost-effective for newbies who want to spend small amounts without being overwhelmed by high fees.

Accessibility is another key advantage of micro-investing sites. They are user-friendly and available via mobile apps, making it handy for newbies to watch their investments and make deals on the go. Automation features like regular payments and round-up transactions make it easy for newbies to create a steady spending habit. Micro-investing focuses on small, gradual purchases, encouraging regular payments. Traditional trading often involves bigger, less frequent deals, which might be scary or difficult for newbies with limited funds.

Choosing a micro-investing platform relies on several factors, including the platform's idea, its features, and the target community. **Acorns** rounds up everyday purchases to the nearest dollar and invests the extra change, giving pre-built portfolios based on risk tolerance. **Robinhood** is a commission-free trading tool that allows users to buy and sell stocks, ETFs, options, and cryptocurrencies without paying traditional exchange fees. **Stash** offers topic investments by selecting ETFs based on specific hobbies or goals, giving portfolios related to areas like technology, green energy, or social effect.

Betterment is a robo-advisor that builds a diverse portfolio based on financial goals and risk tolerance. It uses formulas to automatically adjust your account, giving goal-based trading, tax-efficient methods, and automatic updating.

In conclusion, micro-investing offers numerous benefits for beginners, including low entry hurdles, cost, automation, and a focus on small, increasing investments. By knowing these differences and leveraging the benefits of micro-investing, newbies can start their investment journey with confidence, even with limited financial resources or past experience in the stock market.

The micro-investing platform is a popular trading tool that allows users to trade in stocks, ETFs, cryptocurrencies, and theme portfolios. It gives a range of trading choices, including stocks, ETFs, cryptocurrencies, and theme portfolios. To start an account, users must consider the prices involved with each site, such as account management fees, trade costs, and secret charges.

Investment choices offered by micro-investing sites include stocks, ETFs, cryptocurrencies, and theme portfolios. Account minimums are often needed, and training tools are available to help newbies learn about investments. Customer help services are also rated for answer time and availability.

User-friendliness and accessibility are crucial elements to consider when picking a website. A clean, simple design can improve the overall user experience, especially for newbies. Mobile apps should be available and useful, and customer reviews should be read to understand other buyers' experiences. Accessibility features should be considered for people with disabilities.

To set up a micro-investing account, users need to download the app, register it, provide name verification, and finish a risk assessment. They can also link their bank accounts and payment ways, such as debit card, credit card, or direct transfers. Automatic round-ups can be set up if appropriate, automating micro-investments.

Security steps and personal issues should be considered. Platforms should use encryption and security procedures to protect personal and business information. Ensure the site meets with financial laws and is registered with relevant authorities. Read the platform's privacy policy to understand how your data will be used and shared.

Familiarize yourself with the platform's customer help choices and keep the app updated to the latest version.

Fractional shares are a feature given by micro-investing sites that allow buyers to buy a part of a share rather than a whole share. Benefits of partial shares include cost, diversity, and freedom.

Conclusively, picking a micro-investing platform relies on factors such as prices, funding choices, user-friendliness, and accessibility. By following these steps and ensuring security measures, users can safely set up their micro-investing account while valuing their privacy and data security.

ETFs are financial funds that hold a diverse collection of assets, such as stocks, bonds, or commodities, and are sold on stock markets. They offer diversity, liquidity, and low price rates, making them cost-effective assets.

Individual stocks involve buying shares of a particular company, which can possibly benefit from its growth and profits. Successful individual stock purchases can offer significant profits, power and decision-making, and rewards. Choosing between ETFs and individual stocks relies on the investor's risk level, financial goals, and desire for diversity. ETFs are often favored for their diversity benefits and lower risk, while individual stocks appeal to investors wanting higher possible returns and more control over their investments.

Understanding micro-investment choices is important for micro-investors to make informed decisions when building their investment accounts. Diversification is a risk management technique that involves spreading investments across different assets or asset types. In micro-investing, variety is important as it helps reduce the effect of bad performance from a single investment. By dealing in a range of assets, such as partial shares of different companies, ETFs, and even stocks, micro-investors reduce the overall risk in their portfolio.

A well-diversified strategy might include stock in technology companies, healthcare, consumer items, and foreign markets. Proper asset allocation based on individual risk tolerance and financial goals is key to having a balanced and diverse micro-investment strategy.

Market volatility refers to the fast and significant price changes in financial markets, and micro-investments are not immune to market volatility. Understanding the possible impact of market instability and applying risk management techniques is important for micro-investors to make informed choices, control risks effectively, and work toward achieving their financial goals.

Investment tactics for newbies include round-ups and automatic purchases. Round-ups involve automatically spending extra change from daily transactions, fostering a focused saving habit and possibly leading to significant saves. Automated purchases take minimal effort and remove the need for human payments and decision-making, making it easy for newbies. Incremental growth is also possible as individual round-up numbers build over time.

One-time lump sum trades involve spending a big amount of money at once, such as a bonus or tax return. These trades can profit on chances, possibly yield higher returns, and ease the investment process for some buyers. However, newbies should consider their risk tolerance and diversification before making a lump sum purchase.

Dono-cost averaging (DCA) is a financial method where a trader spends a specific amount of money at regular times, regardless of the asset's price. This method results in getting more shares when prices are low and fewer shares when prices are high, lowering the effects of market instability on the total investment. DCA benefits include risk reduction, focused investment, and possibility for lower average cost.

Portfolio rebalancing includes changing the mix of assets within a financial portfolio to keep desired levels of risk and return. Over time, market changes can cause the share of assets to vary from the initial distribution. Rebalancing ensures that the portfolio stays in line with financial goals and risk tolerance. Benefits of adjusting include risk management, protection of diversity, and improvement of returns.

Rebalancing methods include time-based rebalancing, threshold-based rebalancing, and cash inflows/outflows. Time-based rebalancing includes setting specific time frames to review the portfolio and rebalance it back to the goal allocation. Threshold-based rebalancing rebalances the portfolio when the share of a specific asset type deviates greatly from the goal allocation.

Understanding dollar-cost averaging and portfolio rebalancing enables newbies to adopt effective investment strategies, controlling risk, promoting careful investing, and matching the investment portfolio with financial goals and risk tolerance over the long run.

Investment risks are a major worry that can impact an investor's wealth. Market risk, also known as price risk, refers to the chance of capital losing value due to market changes. Diversification across different asset types can help spread market risk and having a long-term financial perspective can reduce the effect of short-term market swings. Liquidity risk comes when it's difficult to buy or sell a property without causing a major price change. Investing in assets with higher trading numbers and ensuring your investment portfolio includes liquid assets that can be easily bought or sold is important for minimizing this risk.

Credit risk refers to the chance of borrowers failing on their loan obligations. Research the reliability of producers before engaging in bonds or loan platforms to lower exposure to individual credit risks. For lending sites, spread loans across different users to lower exposure to individual credit risks.

Research and due diligence are important in buying. Conduct detailed study on companies, their financial health, business plan, and success records before buying in their stocks. Analyze company reports, financial records, and news stories to consider the business's market place, management team, and industry trends. Evaluate the performance, costs, and past returns of mutual funds, ETFs, or index funds before buying and compare their performance against relevant standards.

In the United States, the Securities Investor Safety Corporation (SIPC) offers minimal safety to customers in case a trading company fails. Understanding the SIPC security limits given by your trading company is important to measure the amount of coverage for your assets. Some trading firms offer extra insurance coverage beyond the SIPC limits and may implement advanced security measures to protect your account from unwanted access and online threats.

By knowing investment risks, conducting thorough research, and being aware of insurance coverage and security measures, investors can make informed choices to minimize risks and improve the safety of their investments.

Tracking and tracking your investments includes getting account records and achievement reports. Brokerage platforms provide regular account records describing investments, transactions, and account amounts, which can be checked and reviewed to ensure correctness and track the general success of your investments. Mobile tools offer real-time information on market prices, account amounts, and individual investment success, allowing you to watch your investments on the go.

Tax consequences and filing rules include tax papers, such as Form 1099, showing financial income, capital gains, and profits. Understanding the date for paying taxes and ensuring you have gotten all necessary tax papers from your trading company can help avoid fines. Tax-efficient tactics like tax-loss harvesting can help lower your total tax bill and improve your after-tax financial profits.

Micro-investing is a strategy that involves making regular contributions to your account, whether through round-ups, automatic payments, or big sum investments. This method allows for growth over time and can increase over time. It is important to have a long-term financial perspective and practice patience to avoid rash choices based on short-term market changes. Regularly reviewing and changing your portfolio is crucial to ensure it fits with your financial goals and risk tolerance. Rebalancing includes changing your asset mix to keep the desired balance between risk and return.

Continuous learning about market trends and economic news is important for making informed business choices.

Diversification across different areas and asset types reduces risk and can help protect your wealth during market downturns. Staying updated with reliable financial news sources, subscriptions to emails, and investment apps that provide real-time market reports can help you make quick investment choices.

Common mistakes to avoid in micro-investing include missing fees and charges, avoiding impulse buying and emotional decision-making, keeping a long-term view, and failing to refresh your portfolio. High costs can significantly eat into profits over time, especially when spending small amounts. Choose platforms with low fees and consider factors like account maintenance fees, transaction fees, and cost rates of funds. Opt for sites that offer reasonable prices and clear fee systems.

Importantly, avoid impulse trading and emotional decision-making by fighting the desire to engage in frequent trading based on short-term market moves. Maintain a long-term view and avoid making financial choices based on emotional reactions to market fluctuations. A well-diversified, long-term financial plan can help manage these changes more successfully.

Neglecting to adjust your portfolio is important to keep the intended variety and risk levels. Schedule regular meetings to measure your portfolio's success and adjust if necessary. Market moves and changes in your financial goals should cause a review of your asset mix. Ignoring the need for adjusting can subject your stock to needless risk.

To build a successful and sustainable investment strategy, be aware of fees, keep a long-term view, and ensure proper portfolio adjustments. For beginners, micro-investing offers a simple and easy way to enter the world of trading. By starting small, being steady, and staying educated, you can gradually build your wealth over time. Additional tools for further learning include books on personal finance and saving, online classes on investing, financial blogs and podcasts, and community groups. Remember, buying is a process that needs constant learning and change. Stay curious, ask questions, and never stop discovering new chances to grow your financial understanding and business account.

Index Fund Investing

Mutual funds or exchange-traded funds (ETFs) aimed at mimicking the performance of a particular market index are known as index funds. By maintaining a diverse portfolio of stocks that closely resembles the composition of the index, they seek to mimic the performance of a certain index, such as the NASDAQ or the S&P 500. Index funds work on the basis of passive management, letting active fund managers choose specific stocks rather than depending on in-depth analysis or stock selection.

Diversification, minimal fees, market performance, and long-term investing are some of the key characteristics of index funds. Holding a wide number of stocks inside the index and distributing the investment across many businesses and industries is how diversification is accomplished. Their passive management strategy, which often has cheaper fees and expenditures compared to actively managed funds, is the reason for their low prices. Index funds provide investors a means to participate in the broad movement of the market by closely mirroring its performance.

Investors with a lengthy time horizon who want steady returns over time can consider index funds. Investors may profit from the market's possible growth and compounding impact by keeping onto their index fund assets. Gaining an understanding of index funds allows investors to investigate this investing choice, which emphasizes low expenses, simplicity, and the possibility of consistent returns depending on the performance of the broader market.

Diversification, low expenses, steady performance, ease of use and accessibility, tax efficiency, and a long-term investing emphasis are among the main benefits of index funds. By distributing risk over many stocks and industries, diversification lessens the effect of a single investment's underwhelming performance. Long-term investor profits are maximized by low expenses resulting from the passive method, which does not need intensive study or active trading. Competitive returns are provided by consistent performance, particularly when one takes into account the reduced costs linked to index funds.

To sum up, index funds provide a reasonable choice for investors who want to mimic the performance of a certain market index. They provide immediate diversity, affordable prices, steady returns, ease of use and accessibility, tax efficiency, and an emphasis on long-term investments. Acknowledging these benefits enables investors to make well-informed choices and see index funds as a worthwhile addition to their investing portfolios.

Investors must choose an index that best fits their investing objectives, risk tolerance, sector and industry emphasis, geographic focus, and performance benchmarks. The S&P 500, NASDAQ Composite, Dow Jones Industrial Average (DJIA), Russell 2000, FTSE 100, DAX, and Nikkei 225 are examples of common stock market indexes. Economists, analysts, and investors often utilize these indexes as crucial markers of market performance to evaluate the general state and trajectory of different global markets.

Investing in index funds has many advantages, such as uniformity, minimal fees and expenses, risk reduction, wide market exposure, and passive vs active management. Wide market exposure lessens the effect of a single investment's bad performance by spreading risk among a number of businesses, industries, and asset classes. Because the strong performance of several equities tends to offset the poor performance of one or a few, diversification helps lessen the effect of unfavorable occurrences on specific firms.

Another benefit of index funds is their low expenses and fees. Investing in actively managed funds yields cheaper transaction and management fees since they incur less operational expenditures than passively managed funds. As a consequence, investors are able to keep a larger portion of their investment returns, which makes index funds an affordable option.

By watching the performance of a certain index, fund managers may avoid continuous oversight, investigation, and decision-making. This approach is known as passive management. Investors may save money by using passive management, which lowers trading expenses and turnover. Passive management achieves consistency because investors may anticipate that the fund's performance will closely resemble the index it monitors. Alternatively, investors may save money with active management, which requires ongoing oversight, investigation, and decision-making by fund managers.

To sum up, investors must choose the appropriate index in order to guarantee that their portfolios reflect their goals, risk tolerance, and personal preferences. A few advantages of index funds include their wide market exposure, risk reduction, minimal expenses and fees, passive management, and stability. Investors may make well-informed investing selections and secure a more prosperous and successful financial future by carefully weighing these variables.

Index funds are good options for retirement savings and other long-term financial objectives because they provide a dependable means of accumulating money over time. Their goal is to mimic the underlying index's performance, which has a track record of growth. Investing in index funds allows investors to take advantage of the growth potential of the market as a whole, which may result in steady returns over time.

Selecting the best index fund involves carefully weighing a number of criteria. Making an educated selection requires careful consideration of a number of factors, including cost analysis, performance review, tax efficiency, fund management experience, liquidity assessment, and compatibility with ESG standards. Through careful research and a clear knowledge of your investing style, you may choose an index fund that complements your financial objectives and creates the foundation for a profitable investing career.

There are many stages involved in setting up an index fund investment:

1. Pick a Reputable Brokerage:
Do your homework and decide on a reputable brokerage
that has a large selection of index funds. Take into account
elements like costs, customer support, user experience, and
potential investment alternatives.

2. Open an Account:
Open an investing account by going to the brokerage's
website or mobile app. Give the appropriate personal and
financial facts, such as your name, address, Social Security
number, and job description.

3. Full Confirmation:
As required by the brokerage, authenticate your identity.
This sometimes entails supplying supplementary
paperwork, such a passport or driver's license, to guarantee
adherence to legal regulations.

4. Establish Finances:
Connect your investing account to your bank account. This
makes it simple for you to send money for both your
original commitment and future donations.

5.Establish Investment Account:
Go to the brokerage's website or mobile app to open an index fund account.

In summary, selecting the appropriate index fund needs careful thought to a number of variables, such as market performance, long-term wealth accumulation, and environmental, social, and governance considerations. Through careful research and a clear knowledge of your investing style, you may choose an index fund that complements your financial objectives and creates the foundation for a profitable investing career.

Investing in index funds is a multi-step procedure that includes selecting the appropriate fund, putting up the first investment, establishing automatic installments, monitoring and modifying contributions, and reinvested dividends. To successfully construct an index fund portfolio that meets your financial goals, you must follow these steps.

When investing in index funds, volatility and market risks are important factors to take into account. The performance of index funds may be impacted by market movements, which might result in brief drops in the value of your investment. There are limitations to diversification as well since index funds are still subject to the performance of the market as a whole. It's also crucial to take fund performance variation and tracking faults into account.

It's important to understand capital gains and dividends since some investors depend on them for income, while others may opt to reinvest their payouts for compound growth. Capital gains distributions have tax ramifications that should be taken into consideration. Tax-efficient index funds are especially crucial for taxable accounts and may improve after-tax returns.

Rebalancing and long-term planning are crucial components of an efficient index fund investment management strategy. Investors may take advantage of compounding's strength, which creates returns on prior returns and eventually leads to exponential growth, by adopting a long-term view. Another reason to ride out market volatility is that it allows investors to maintain their investments during bear markets without giving in to impulse buys or sells.

Maintaining asset allocation, purchasing cheap, selling high, and modifying the portfolio correspondingly are all part of periodic portfolio rebalancing. By using a disciplined strategy, investors may take advantage of market opportunities and avoid being overexposed to assets that are overpriced.

To sum up, while investing in index funds, one must carefully evaluate the risks associated with the market, tracking mistakes, and tax consequences. Effective index fund management requires regular monitoring, comprehension of the fund's performance in relation to the index, and consideration of tax consequences. Investors may take advantage of compounding, weather market turbulence, and stick to their investment objective by taking a long-term view.

Regardless of market circumstances, the Dollar-Cost Averaging (DCA) approach entails investing a predetermined amount of money at regular periods. This lessens the effect of market volatility on the whole investment and assists investors in resisting the urge to attempt to time the market. By distributing the investment throughout a range of market situations, DCA lowers the risk associated with placing large bets during market peaks. By taking emotion out of investing choices, it also encourages emotional discipline by making it simpler to adhere to a long-term investment strategy and remain invested.

Through the adoption of a long-term outlook, consistent portfolio rebalancing, and the use of dollar-cost averaging, investors may effectively manage market intricacies, curtail risks, and systematically strive towards accomplishing their financial objectives. These methods provide a methodical approach to investing in index funds, encouraging stability and steady growth over time.

Capital gains taxes and dividends are among the tax ramifications and reporting associated with index fund investment. When a fund sells assets at a profit, capital gains are taxable, and investors must pay capital gains taxes when they sell fund shares at a profit. For investors in index funds, tax-efficient tactics include long-term holding, harvesting tax losses, and using tax-advantaged accounts such as 401(k) plans or IRAs.

Form 1099-DIV, maintaining track of index fund transactions, speaking with a tax expert, and comprehending the tax ramifications of index fund investments are among the paperwork and reporting needs. Overtrading, market timing, disregarding expenditure ratios and fees, and failing to account for possible hidden expenses are common mistakes to avoid.

To sum up, DCA is an organized method of investing in index funds that supports tax efficiency, steady growth, and stability. Investors should get advice from a tax adviser and be mindful of possible dangers. Investors may maximize their after-tax returns and make well-informed choices while efficiently managing their tax obligations by maintaining correct records, applying tax-efficient tactics, and understanding the tax implications of index fund investments.

When investing in index funds, diversification is essential since it distributes risk throughout a variety of industries, asset classes, and geographical areas, improving portfolio stability. If a single sector or index performs badly, an over dependence on it may result in large losses. Another crucial factor is overconcentration, which may increase losses in down markets.

Over time, if you don't rebalance your portfolio, you may become overexposed to particular assets and face unexpected hazards. By being aware of these potential hazards, investors may steer clear of needless expenses, make educated judgments, and have a diverse, well-balanced portfolio. You may reduce these risks and improve the overall performance of your index fund investments by maintaining discipline, keeping an eye on long-term objectives, and routinely evaluating your investing approach.

Books like **"The Little Book of Common Sense Investing"** by John C. Bogle, **"A Random Walk Down Wall Street"** by Burton G. Malkiel, and **"Common Sense on Mutual Funds"** by John C. Bogle are recommended reading for anybody interested in index funds. You may find online seminars and classes on index funds at Bogleheads, Investopedia, and Coursera. For investors in index funds, financial blogs and podcasts may be a great way to get insightful information and remain current on the newest trends and best practices in the field.

Diversification, low expenses, a long-term outlook, discipline and patience, and sticking to your investment strategy through ups and downs in the market are all important index fund investing concepts. Novice investors may take advantage of index funds' ease of use, inexpensive charges, and wide market exposure, seeing market swings as chances to stick to their investing strategy.

A professional financial adviser may be consulted, online groups can be joined, and investing and personal finance education can be pursued as additional resources for support and community involvement. These sites may provide tailored advice and support in making difficult financial choices.

To sum up, index fund investment provides a dependable and efficient means of accumulating money over time. Investors, particularly novices, may successfully manage the financial markets and work toward their long-term financial objectives by following the fundamental principles, keeping discipline, and seeking guidance when necessary. Happy making purchases!

Real Estate Crowdfunding

A contemporary investing technique called real estate crowdfunding enables people to combine their funds online and purchase real estate. By allowing smaller investors to participate in bigger projects that were previously only available to institutional investors or high-net-worth people, this idea democratizes real estate investing. A real estate venture can be funded by a number of relatively small individual investors pooling their money together. This allows investors to diversify their holdings, potentially earn returns through property appreciation or rental income, and take advantage of the real estate market without having to deal with the hassles of property management or large capital requirements.

Real estate crowdfunding works with a variety of investment formats, including debt and equity investments, in which investors lend money to the developer of the project or become part owners of the property themselves. Diverse risk and return profiles provided by each model enable investors to choose investments that are in line with their financial objectives. This creative method of investing in real estate opens doors for novices, allowing them to investigate the market and maybe earn passive income. As a result, it's a desirable side job for those who want to gradually accumulate money and diversify their sources of income.

The advantages of using real estate crowdfunding as a side gig include the ability to access a variety of real estate assets, professional management, lower entry barriers, diversification of investments, potential for high returns, liquidity and exit strategies, and possible risks and considerations. When thinking about real estate crowdfunding as a side gig, some possible dangers and factors to take into account include market volatility, project-specific risks, lack of liquidity, regulatory and legal concerns, and platform dependability.

A few well-known platforms for real estate crowdfunding include **RealtyMogul, Fundrise, Crowdstreet, PeerStreet, and RealtyShares**. A range of investment alternatives, including development projects and eREITs (real estate investment trusts), are available on Fundrise's user-friendly platform. For accredited and non-accredited investors, **RealtyMogul** offers a platform with a variety of investment choices, including commercial real estate, multifamily housing, and retail spaces. With an emphasis on commercial real estate investments, **Crowdstreet** links financiers with projects of institutional caliber and provides a wide selection of assets, including office buildings, hotels, and industrial spaces. **PeerStreet** is an expert in short-term loans secured by real estate, specializing in real estate debt investments.

RealityShares demonstrated the potential variety of real estate crowdfunding initiatives; but, as of November 2018, the company has discontinued operations. By being aware of these advantages and disadvantages, people are better equipped to decide whether to pursue real estate crowdfunding as a side gig.

Through equity investments, investors may make returns through the appreciation of their property and rental revenue, so becoming partial owners of a project or real estate. Although there is a chance for larger profits with this technique, there is also a greater risk since property prices might change. In contrast, debt investments include investors lending money to real estate developers or borrowers in order to finance real estate developments and generate interest payments. Compared to equity investments, debt investments have less risk and more predictable returns, but they could not have as much upside potential if the value of the property increases dramatically.

For those considering real estate crowdfunding as a side gig, it's critical to comprehend these platforms and investment schemes. Investors may choose solutions that are in line with their financial aims and preferences since each platform and investment type accommodates a range of risk tolerances and investment goals.

Real estate projects fall into three categories: development, commercial, and residential. Residential projects include buildings designed for single-family homes, townhouses, apartments, condos, and housing communities, among other structures intended for use by people and families. With a concentration on buildings utilized for business, commercial developments, particularly those located in prestigious business areas, provide diversity and the possibility of greater rental returns. In development projects, buildings are built or refurbished for a variety of uses, such as new residential or commercial developments or the transformation of existing properties into higher-value assets.

Real estate crowdfunding raises a number of legal and regulatory issues, such as tax ramifications, investor protections, due diligence and transparency requirements, securities laws, and investor accreditation. While investor accreditation enables investors to access a wider choice of investment possibilities, securities rules require platforms and investors to conform with securities laws and regulations relevant in their country. While rules establish investor protection measures including disclosure requirements, dispute resolution processes, and investment amount restrictions, due diligence guarantees openness and gives investors accurate information.

Visit the official website of the crowdfunding platform, register, provide identification, arrange financing, and finish your profile in order to establish an account. Examining project specifics, evaluating risk and return, perusing investor feedback, and looking through potential projects are all part of the process of investigating investment prospects. The minimum and maximum investment quantities, as well as the diversification of assets and the investigation of properties and project developers, are among the investment amounts and conditions.

Researching the developer's history, the location of the property, financial estimates, legal and regulatory compliance, and the platform's reputation are all part of due diligence. Reputable platforms uphold openness, provide safeguards for investors, and carry out exhaustive due diligence on projects that are posted. When taking part in real estate crowdfunding initiatives, investors may reduce risk, make well-informed choices, and increase their chances of success by following these guidelines.

Crowdfunding for real estate is a vibrant and competitive sector where investors want to finance projects that match their financial objectives. Investors must carry out due investigation and carefully choose investments that are suited to their financial objectives in order to guarantee a successful crowdfunding experience.

Tracking returns, project updates, and the platform's communication channels are all part of keeping an eye on the success of your investments. Investors should check the data and performance summaries the platform provides by routinely logging into their account. Updates from the platform and developers should also be used to keep them updated on the status of the project. Email alerts and mobile app alerts are examples of communication channels that may be used to notify investors of important project developments, construction milestones, or schedule adjustments.

Long-term growth depends on how distributions—like dividends, interest payments, and profit sharing—are handled. While manual reinvestment enables investors to diversify their portfolio and adjust it to their changing financial objectives, platforms may provide automated reinvestment alternatives where revenues are reinvested into new projects or current assets. When reinvesting profits, investors should think about the tax consequences and speak with a tax expert to understand how reinvested income is treated tax-wise so they can plan their reinvestment strategy appropriately.

Real estate crowdfunding entails a number of risks and risk management strategies, such as interest rate variations, market demand fluctuations, project-specific hazards, and market volatility. Variations in interest rates may result in increased borrowing costs for developers, and market volatility might impact possible returns on investments. Risks unique to a project could include variations in market demand, difficulties with regulations, and delays in development. By dispersing investments among a number of platforms, initiatives, and conditions and agreements, diversification techniques may reduce risk.

In the realm of real estate crowdfunding, investors must comprehend terms and agreements in order to make wise investment choices. Aside from paying close attention to profit-sharing plans, exit options, and deadlines, investors should thoroughly study and comprehend all terms, conditions, and agreements pertaining to their investments. If required, they should also get legal counsel. It's crucial for investors to have open lines of contact with platforms and developers in order to evaluate the project's development and make well-informed judgments.

Real estate crowdfunding requires time management, diversification of income sources, goal-setting that is reasonable, and knowledge of the tax consequences on crowdfunding profits in order to be balanced with other side projects or full-time employment. By doing this, investors may help achieve their long-term financial objectives and properly manage the risks related to real estate crowdfunding.

In conclusion, market risks, project-specific difficulties, and tax ramifications must all be carefully considered before making a real estate crowdfunding investment. Investors may optimize their prospective profits and make well-informed selections by being aware of these aspects.

An increasing number of people are taking advantage of real estate crowdfunding as a means of making passive income from their assets. But it's crucial to comprehend the tax ramifications of real estate crowdfunding profits and take into account any possible deductions associated with these investments.

Real estate crowdfunding money may be subject to income taxes, therefore it's important to appropriately declare your profits to the government. Profits from the sale of real estate crowdfunding investments may also be subject to capital gains tax, so it's important to understand the applicable rates and guidelines. If you want to maximize your tax approach, think about speaking with a tax expert.

Real estate investment-related tax deductions may reduce taxable income and increase after-tax profits. Through dividends and interest payments, real estate crowdfunding may provide reliable revenue streams that can be utilized to invest in income-producing ventures to generate steady cash flow. Reinvesting profits into new ventures has the potential to increase returns over time and provide a steady stream of passive income if done as part of a long-term investment plan.

In order to get the most out of real estate crowdfunding as a side gig or long-term investment plan, you need to balance your activities with other responsibilities, be aware of how your profits will be taxed, and use crowdfunding to generate passive income. Participating in online communities, attending webinars and seminars, signing up for platform-specific forums, and continuing your education with books, blogs, and podcasts are all ways to foster community participation and learning in real estate crowdfunding.

When it comes to real estate crowdfunding, diversity, diligence, ongoing education, and community involvement are essential guidelines for novices. Spreading investments among a variety of projects helps to reduce risk and improve portfolio stability. When making investment choices, due diligence is doing extensive study on platforms, developers, and projects in order to fully comprehend the risks and possible rewards involved. Using books, blogs, podcasts, webinars, and other online resources to remain current on legal requirements, investing methods, and market trends is known as continuous learning. Setting reasonable objectives, staying away from overcommitting, and managing your real estate crowdfunding endeavors in addition to other side projects or full-time work are all part of investing balance.

Tax issues include knowing how your profits will be taxed and working with tax experts to maximize your tax plan. Participating in the community enables you to grow your network and get knowledge from seasoned investors.

Starting a real estate crowdfunding campaign is a big step toward achieving financial stability and generating passive income. Accepting the concepts of diversity, diligence, ongoing education, and community involvement can help you successfully negotiate the intricacies of the real estate crowdfunding market.

Explore reliable real estate crowdfunding platforms, go to local real estate events, look for mentorship from seasoned investors, and speak with financial advisors, tax experts, and real estate investment-focused lawyers as extra resources and support for continuing learning and development. Keep in mind that your experience with real estate crowdfunding is an ongoing educational process. With commitment and initiative, you can turn it into a lucrative side gig that will help you reach your financial goals.

Dropshipping

Finding lucrative dropshipping niches is essential to success since it enables you to market to a certain group of people with goods they are more likely to be interested in purchasing. This may help you generate more revenue in the long run by increasing sales and conversion rates. Think about your hobbies and areas of expertise, examine market trends, assess competitors, look at profit margins, and think about the feasibility of your product while looking for lucrative niches.

Pet supplies, fashion accessories, home décor, technology, and health and beauty items are a few successful dropshipping areas. Because individuals usually keep spending money on their furry pals even during economic downturns, pet products are comparatively recession-proof. Home décor provides a large selection of items at various price ranges, while fashion accessories are popular since they are reasonably priced and easy to transport. Electronics are a costly product that dropshippers may profit from greatly, but they are also quite competitive.

Establishing a trustworthy supplier network is crucial to the success of any dropshipping company. Order fulfillment for your clients is the responsibility of your suppliers, thus it's critical to choose dependable, efficient, and trustworthy partners. Reliable suppliers may raise brand recognition, save expenses, and boost customer happiness. Strong supplier relationships provide you the assurance that your clients will get their purchases promptly and undamaged, which makes them happy and more willing to do business with you again.

Investigate potential dropshipping suppliers by looking through internet reviews, visiting the supplier's website, and getting in touch with their customer support department. Before agreeing to deal with them, get samples of their items so you can check the quality. Engage in price negotiations with your suppliers; the more you order, the more power you will own. After agreements are agreed upon, get everything in writing to safeguard you in the event that issues arise later.

Maintaining good supplier relationships requires proactive behavior, timely bill payment, and frequent contact. Inform your suppliers of any changes to your company's operations and inventory requirements, and take prompt action to resolve any issues that may arise with an order. Long-term success depends on your ability to pay your payments on time. With the aid of these pointers, you may choose and oversee trustworthy dropshipping suppliers that will support the growth of your company.

In conclusion, finding lucrative dropshipping niches is critical to your business as it enables you to target a certain market with goods that people are more likely to be interested in purchasing. Establishing a trustworthy network of suppliers is essential to your company's success since it guarantees that your goods will be delivered on schedule, in excellent shape, and with a high caliber.

Any dropshipping company that wants to increase sales, improve conversion rates, and increase exposure must have product listings. Businesses may draw in more consumers and entice them to make purchases by exhibiting their items to prospective clients. Businesses can utilize analytics tools, strategic keyword use, attractive product names, thorough descriptions, high-quality photos, competitive pricing, calls to action that are obvious, mobile device optimization, and frequent updates to improve their product listings. Positive customer reviews are also important.

Customer service is just as important to any dropshipping company's success as product listing optimization. Good customer experiences are cultivated by exceptional customer service, which also promotes repeat business and increases brand loyalty. Customers who are happy with your shop are more likely to return back and refer others to it.

Another key benefit of dropshipping is building your brand's image. Goodwill and online testimonials from satisfied consumers may help you build your brand's reputation and draw in new clients. Being proactive in providing customer care may help avoid bad reviews, which can seriously harm your business and turn off prospective consumers. When customers get timely and efficient customer care, they may get the information and help they need to make well-informed purchase choices. Sales growth and improved conversion rates may result from this.

In dropshipping, getting insightful feedback is particularly crucial as consumer interactions reveal preferences for certain products, expectations for certain services, and areas in need of development. Dropshipping organizations should emphasize response times, set up various lines of contact, address concerns with empathy, go above and above, empower their customer service personnel, and always strive for continuous improvement in order to guarantee outstanding client happiness.

1. Establish various lines of communication:
Give your consumers many ways to contact you, including social media, phone, live chat, and email. Give them the option to choose their favorite way for quick and easy help.

2. Make response times a priority:
Establish explicit deadlines for answering consumer questions, then aim to achieve or surpass them. Show them that you appreciate their time and concerns by getting back to them quickly and effectively.

3. Treat problems with empathy:
Address client complaints with compassion and understanding, expressing regret for any difficulties caused, and cooperating to find solutions.

4. Go above and beyond:
To show your dedication to client pleasure, go above and beyond by going above and beyond and giving proactive help, extra product information, or a little token of appreciation.

5. Invest in the training and empowerment of your customer service staff: Give your staff the tools they need to efficiently manage client interactions.

6. Keep an eye on customer satisfaction indicators and solicit feedback to pinpoint areas that need work. Then, fine-tune your customer service tactics to surpass consumer expectations and maintain a customer-centric philosophy.

To sum up, providing great customer service involves more than simply fixing problems; it also entails developing rapport, encouraging trust, and producing a satisfying brand experience that will entice clients to return. Businesses may build a devoted client base and promote long-term success in their dropshipping company by putting a high priority on customer happiness.

Social media networks are becoming an essential resource for dropshipping companies, providing a focused and economical way to reach new clients, highlight items, and increase revenue. These platforms provide companies the ability to target particular audiences based on their demographics, hobbies, and online activity thanks to their extensive targeting choices. This strategy makes sure that the correct individuals get marketing messages and raises the possibility of conversion.

Social media offers a special chance to establish a powerful online presence, which increases brand recognition as well. Dropshipping companies may establish a distinctive brand identity and draw in new clients by regularly posting interesting content, communicating with followers, and working with influencers.

Social media marketing is very inexpensive when compared to conventional marketing techniques like advertising, enabling companies to increase their brand awareness without having to make substantial financial commitments. Another benefit is direct client connection, which is made possible by apps like Instagram and TikTok that allow users to communicate directly with both current and new customers. Another benefit is that visual storytelling is made possible by the highly visual nature of platforms like Instagram and TikTok, which let companies present their goods in an interesting and enticing way.

Social media platforms also provide real-time analytics tools that let companies monitor the effectiveness of their marketing initiatives, gauge audience involvement, and learn more about their preferences. Businesses should know their target, provide high-quality content, employ influencer marketing, conduct social media competitions, interact with followers, use relevant hashtags, and routinely check social media analytics in order to use social media platforms for dropshipping marketing efficiently.

Dropshipping companies may successfully use social media to raise brand recognition, attract traffic to their shop, and improve sales by leveraging social media platforms carefully and producing interesting content catered to their target demographic. In order to improve client satisfaction, encourage repeat business, improve the entire customer experience, and increase sales, a user-friendly website and a simple checkout procedure are also necessary.

A website that is easy to use is essential for making a good first impression and assisting clients as they purchase. Easy navigation, eye-catching design, mobile optimization, quick loading times, lucid product information, social proof, and a simplified checkout procedure are all essential components of a user-friendly website. These components contribute to less friction and cart abandonment, which raises consumer happiness and encourages repeat business and profitable dropshipping.

The best pricing plan for your dropshipping company will depend on a number of factors, including competitive analysis, product quality considerations, profit margin maintenance, dynamic pricing, psychological pricing, tiered pricing, promotional pricing, performance monitoring, product positioning, and customer value proposition. Examine the pricing tactics of your rivals, evaluate their advantages and disadvantages, and utilize this knowledge to set your rates competitively while preserving a healthy profit margin.

greater-quality items tend to fetch greater costs, since perceived worth and pricing potential are directly influenced by product quality. To keep your profit margin within goal, figure out how much your product costs, overhead, and intended profit are. Use dynamic pricing techniques to modify prices in response to current market circumstances, shifts in demand, and pricing tactics of competitors. Use psychological pricing strategies, such as setting product prices at $19.99 rather than $20, to gently influence customers' choices to buy.

By providing discounts for big purchases, tier pricing schemes may promote larger orders and boost total income.

Make smart use of promotional pricing to increase sales and draw in new clients. Track sales information, client comments, and industry developments to keep an eye on performance and adjust prices for optimal profit.

Analyze where your product fits in the market and if luxury or premium items are more expensive, or whether more affordable, basic items are needed. Recognize the value your goods provide to the market and use this to support higher pricing since they are seen to be worth it.

As consumer preferences, competition dynamics, and market circumstances change, effective pricing strategies should too. Maintaining profitability and expanding your dropshipping company requires you to constantly assess and modify your pricing strategy. Dropshipping companies may greatly improve the general customer experience by putting these tactics into practice. This will raise customer happiness, encourage repeat business, and result in a profitable dropshipping endeavor.

Chapter 2

High-Return Side Hustle Investment Strategies

Starting A Blog

In the world of blogging, picking a niche or topic that excites you is essential for a number of reasons: knowledge and experience, sustainability and motivation, attraction of target audience, personal growth and fulfillment, SEO optimization, and long-term sustainability. You may better target your material to a certain readership, raise the possibility that your writing will speak to their needs and interests, and establish your expertise and reputation in that industry by focusing on a particular niche or area of interest.

Identifying your niche is crucial for a number of reasons, including helping you stand out from the crowd, identifying certain rivals within it, promoting a feeling of community among your readers, increasing the visibility of your blog in search engine results, and guaranteeing long-term viability. Embracing your hobbies and identifying your specialty can help you connect with a specific audience, become recognized as an authority, and create a vibrant community around your interests.

In the world of blogging, creating an engaging opening is similar to creating a welcoming storefront. It acts as your readers' first point of contact, piqueing their interest and luring them to read more of your blog's material. The following advice will help you write an engaging opening that makes your readers want to read on:

1. Grab readers' attention right away: Begin with an attention-grabbing introduction that captures their interest in the first phrase. A compelling question, an unexpected fact, or a captivating story might grab their attention right away and entice them to read further.

2. Establish your voice and introduce yourself: By doing so, you may let your individuality come through. Give visitors a flavor of what makes your blog interesting and different by sharing your background, experience, and hobbies.

3.Establish the tenor and fashion: Whether it's witty, educational, or inspiring, your introduction should capture the general feel and look of your site.

4. Emphasize the value offering. Describe the information, amusement, or inspiration that your blog provides for readers.

5. Close with a call to action: Make sure your call to action is obvious to entice readers to take action. Urge people to share

your information with others, leave comments on your postings, and subscribe to your site.

In conclusion, choosing a niche or topic that excites you is essential to blogging success. You may develop a distinctive and compelling blog that connects with your audience by concentrating on subjects that excite you, expanding your knowledge and skill set, and encouraging a feeling of community. Creating an engaging blog that engages readers and sets the setting for a successful trip can be achieved by following these steps. Creating a captivating beginning is similar to creating a welcoming storefront.

For bloggers to keep their blogs interesting and consistent, a content schedule is an essential tool. It makes it possible to prepare and schedule blog entries ahead of time, guaranteeing structure and focus. A content schedule may be made using programs like Asana, Trello, and Google schedule, which encourages visitors to stay on your site and return for more.

Selecting a format, coming up with ideas, planning articles, and marketing postings on social media are all steps in the creation of a content calendar. Content calendars may also be managed via content management systems (CMS) that have content calendar features integrated into them.

Using a content schedule can help you be more productive, write better blogs, attract more readers, boost SEO, and feel less stressed. You may enhance your blog in a number of ways by taking the effort to organize and schedule your work ahead of time.

Successful blogging requires creating a community around your site. By replying to messages, addressing queries, and taking part in conversations, you demonstrate to your readers that you appreciate their opinions and would want to create a community around your site. Here are a few strategies for interacting with your viewer:

1. Leave a comment on each of your blog entries, even if it's only to express gratitude. This demonstrates to your readers that you value their opinions and are paying attention to what they have to say.

2. Provide well-considered and educational answers to queries, demonstrating to your audience your expertise in the subject and willingness to impart it.

3. Take part in debates on other websites and your blog to establish connections with other bloggers and get new followers.

Along with following these suggestions, you can interact with your audience by promoting your blog pieces on social media and asking followers to share them. While doing polls and surveys may help you get reader input and discover more about their interests, holding freebies and competitions can create excitement and draw in new readers. It takes time and work to develop a following for your blog, but the effort is worthwhile. A devoted audience will increase your chances of drawing in new ones and retaining current ones so they come back for more.

Interacting with your readers will boost their number, as well as the quality of your site, SEO, and level of pleasure. You can create a vibrant community of readers who will stick with your blog for years to come by taking the time to get to know them.

An essential step in increasing your blog's visibility to search engines like Google is search engine optimization, or SEO. You may improve the likelihood that people will find your blog entries when they are searching for information on the subjects you write about by adhering to fundamental SEO guidelines.

To find relevant terms people use to seek for information on the subjects you write about, keyword research is crucial.

Include keywords in all areas of your blog entries, such as the title, meta description, and body of the content. Since article titles and meta descriptions are the first things readers will see when your blog posts show up in search results, make sure they are optimized. Create backlinks to your blog from other websites by guest posting, submitting it to directories, and engaging in online discussion boards.

Make sure your blog is mobile-friendly
: With more people accessing the internet via smartphones and tablets, it's important to ensure that readers can access your information on a variety of devices. To improve your chances of getting readers to view your blog pieces, share them on social media.

Make use of photos and videos:
These media may enhance the readability of your writing, add visual interest to your blog entries, and raise your search engine rankings. To assist search engines like Google and Bing in indexing your material, submit your blog to them.

Be patient: SEO takes time, and you may not see returns from your efforts for months or even years. But you may ultimately raise your blog's search engine ranks and draw in more viewers if you're persistent and patient.

Multimedia components like photos, videos, and infographics may greatly improve your content and increase the overall attractiveness of your site. In addition to captivating your audience, multimedia also accommodates a variety of learning styles, so your message will be understood by a larger number of readers.

It is inherently possible for multimedia features to capture interest and elicit participation, which enhances visual stimulation and facilitates comprehension.

They also accommodate different learning methods, which makes a larger readership interested in your site. Using multimedia in your blog also helps with visual storytelling. An picture used correctly may elicit feelings, establish the tone of a story, and communicate ideas that words cannot. Infographics make it simpler for readers to understand and remember important takeaways by condensing complicated information into visually attractive pictures. Videos are outstanding storytelling tools that may successfully catch attention and convey captivating messages because of their unique blend of pictures, audio, and movement.

Multimedia integration is essentially a calculated tactic that improves reader engagement, supports a range of learning preferences, fortifies narrative, increases search engine optimization, and expands the scope of your writing. Your blog may become much more than just a collection of text by using multimedia. It can become a lively, interesting, and educational platform that captivates readers and makes a lasting impact.

Creating An Online Course

Determining an online course's target audience is essential to its success. Understanding the characteristics, experiences, goals, and obstacles of your students can help you customize the course material, delivery strategies, and whole learning process to meet their unique requirements.

Think about your target audience's prior knowledge, interests, motivations, pain points, issues, and queries as you determine their skill level. You may design an online course that connects with your target audience and assists them in achieving their goals by giving these things serious thought.

Establish measurable and achievable learning objectives for an online course by starting with the big picture, breaking the goal down into smaller, more focused objectives, using action verbs, keeping the objectives achievable, aligning them with assessments, clearly communicating the objectives in the course materials and outline, and reviewing and improving them on a regular basis.

For both the teacher and the students, well-defined learning goals act as a road map, guaranteeing that the course is targeted, efficient, and in line with the intended results. The creation of captivating material is essential for holding students' interest and promoting an active online learning environment. You may maximize information retention and overall engagement by optimizing learning styles and preferences via the use of varied multimedia components and instructional techniques.

Leveraging the power of video, introducing interactive quizzes, using downloadable resources, incorporating different teaching methods, introducing storytelling elements, encouraging active participation, incorporating visual appeal, and audience-tailored content are some effective strategies to take into consideration.

In conclusion, determining the target audience for an online course entails taking into account the participants' difficulties, motivations, interests, and skill level. You may design a dynamic online learning environment that accommodates a range of learning preferences and styles by adopting specific learning goals, adding multimedia components, and including narrative aspects. By putting these techniques into practice, you may produce interesting and useful online course material that increases information retention, adapts to different learning styles, and improves the overall learning experience for your students.

Use these guidelines to create an online course platform that is easy to use:

1. Select a trustworthy LMS (learning management system): Choose a reputable supplier with a sizable user base and a track record of success. Examine the LMS features to make sure they provide a smooth learning environment and correspond with the needs of your course. Put accessibility first by selecting an LMS that puts an emphasis on usability and makes it possible for students with disabilities to interact and browse the course material in an efficient manner.

2. Use simple instructions and guidance: To help students navigate the course content, include visual clues, breadcrumbs, and straightforward navigation.

3. Promote a logical and consistent learning environment by using the same vocabulary throughout the course, creating a consistent interface, and arranging the course contents rationally.

4. Give accessibility and inclusiveness a priority. To accommodate various learning styles, make sure the product is compatible with a variety of devices, take into account

different learning methods, and include multimedia components.

5. Constantly evaluate and enhance: Regularly compile learner input, examine use statistics, and modify and enhance the platform in response to input and usage data. Dedicated discussion boards, live Q&A sessions, group projects, virtual breakout rooms, peer review activities, social media encouragement, and gamification elements can all be used to promote communication and cooperation among students in an online course.

6. Encourage icebreakers and introductions: To assist students get to know one another, make connections, and develop a feeling of community, facilitate icebreaker activities and introductions at the start of the course.

7. Establish clear standards and expectations: Clearly state what is expected of participants and interactions, with a focus on polite dialogue, involvement, and helpful criticism.

8. Consistently promote and acknowledge participation: To create a welcoming and stimulating learning atmosphere, actively encourage students to take part in debates, group projects, and other interactive activities.

You may improve your students' overall learning experience, build a sense of community, and promote connection and teamwork by putting these methods into practice.

Effective online learning requires the inclusion of constructive criticism and frequent evaluations. Through assessments, teachers may assess students' progress, pinpoint their areas of strength and weakness, and provide individualized instruction. Feedback that is constructive clears misunderstandings, inspires learners, and promotes ongoing development. Use a range of assessment techniques, such as essays, simulations, case studies, quizzes, and project-based tasks, to efficiently integrate evaluations and helpful criticism into online courses.

To make sure that the assessment is in line with the course material and learning objectives, clear instructions and goals should be given. Specific areas of strength and weakness should be addressed in prompt and constructive feedback. Each student should get personalized feedback that takes into account their own skills, weaknesses, and learning preferences. Different learning styles and preferences may be accommodated by using several feedback sources.

To make sure students comprehend the instructor's recommendations and can apply them to their learning, it is essential to promote discussion and clarification about the feedback they get. Self-assessment tools must to be included in the curriculum to motivate students to evaluate their own development, pinpoint areas that need work, and establish individual learning objectives. Activities involving peer evaluation should encourage critical thinking, provide constructive criticism, and foster a feeling of shared accountability for learning.

Stressing the function of feedback as a continuous learning process rather than a performance evaluation, feedback as a learning process should be prioritized. These techniques will let you add evaluations and helpful criticism to your online courses in an efficient manner that will improves student motivation and learning outcomes while encouraging ongoing development.

For your online course to reach its target audience and draw in new students, effective promotion is crucial. Think about putting in place a thorough marketing plan that uses a range of platforms and methods. The following are important tactics to think about: determining your target market, crafting an engaging course description, building a marketing website, utilizing social media, focusing on online forums and communities, collaborating with bloggers and influencers, providing early bird discounts and promotions, utilizing email marketing campaigns, organizing webinars and online events, search engine optimizing, running targeted ads, getting feedback and acting upon it, monitoring and assessing marketing performance, and keeping a consistent marketing presence across all channels.

By putting these tactics into practice, you can reach your target audience, market your online course successfully, and draw in new students who will find your insightful material beneficial.

Investing In Cryptocurrency

Cryptocurrency is a kind of virtual or digital money that is decentralized—that is, not governed by banks or governments—and employs encryption for protection. It may be used to pay for products and services and is often exchanged on decentralized marketplaces.

Satoshi Nakamoto launched Bitcoin, the first and most popular cryptocurrency, in 2009. Because encryption is used, it is both secure and decentralized. Blockchain-based Ethereum is another well-known cryptocurrency that was developed in 2015 by Vitalik Buterin. Cryptocurrencies are powered by blockchain technology, a distributed record that makes transactions hard to tamper with.

Because of variables related to supply and demand, the price of Bitcoin is erratic and subject to sudden fluctuations. The demand for Ethereum is fueled by elements including its rising popularity and usage as a store of wealth, whereas the supply of Bitcoin remains restricted. Sending Bitcoin involves transaction fees that are based on the amount of the transaction and the condition of the network, and they may be quite expensive when there is a lot of network congestion.

A software application called a Bitcoin wallet is used to hold private keys, which are necessary in order to access Bitcoin. Hardware, software, and mobile wallets are among the several kinds of Bitcoin wallets that are available. The process of adding transactions to the Bitcoin blockchain and validating them is known as "mining," for which miners are paid in Bitcoin in exchange for their labor. Ethereum mining is a competitive process where miners solve challenging mathematical puzzles using specialized gear.

It is essential to comprehend blockchain technology while making cryptocurrency investments. The project, team, market potential, tokenomics, and cryptocurrency risk are important variables to take into account. It is crucial to comprehend the objectives of the bitcoin initiative. The cryptocurrency's development crew need to be skilled and competent to carry out the project's goals. The market opportunity need to take the target market's size and possible use cases into account. The allocation and application of cryptocurrency tokens, or tokenomics, must also be taken into account.

Investing in cryptocurrency carries a significant risk, and success is not guaranteed. It's crucial to only make cryptocurrency investments that you fully understand and can tolerate the risk of.

One well-liked and safe method of managing and storing bitcoin is via cryptocurrency wallets. Hardware wallets are physical devices that keep private keys offline, making them almost impenetrable to hackers. Examples of these wallets include the Trezor Model T, Ledger Nano S, and KeepKey. On the other side, software wallets—such as Exodus, MetaMask, and MyEtherWallet—are more user-friendly but less secure. On the other hand, institutional investors and seasoned traders use mobile wallets, which are programs that can be downloaded and used on mobile devices.

Selecting a trustworthy cryptocurrency exchange is essential to guaranteeing both a seamless trading experience and the safety of your money. Exchanges that are well-known include Kraken, Binance, and Coinbase. Check an exchange's security measures, user feedback, and regulatory compliance before choosing one. Security precautions like two-factor authentication, cold storage for user cash, and frequent security audits are important things to think about.

It's important to start small and make smart investments before making any bitcoin investments. Start small and give yourself time to become comfortable with the ins and outs of trading and the dynamics of the market. Put knowledge before fast money by studying blockchain technology, doing in-depth project analysis, and keeping up with industry advancements. Spread your money among a variety of assets, looking at more recent ventures with solid foundations as well as well-known cryptocurrencies with plenty of untapped potential.

By investing within your means, never investing money you cannot afford to lose, and using risk management techniques like stop-loss orders to minimize possible losses and avoiding excessive leverage, you may practice prudence and risk management. Seek advice and remain educated by participating in online forums, going to instructional sessions, and checking reliable information sources.

To sum up, investing in cryptocurrencies has risks by nature and should be done so with discipline, patience, and a well-thought-out plan. Diversifying your cryptocurrency portfolio and starting small may assist to lower overall risk and offset market swings. Recall that there are dangers associated with investing in cryptocurrencies, and previous performance does not guarantee future outcomes.

For bitcoin investors to reduce risk and increase their chances of success, diversification is an essential tactic. Investors might possibly take advantage of opportunities in different segments of the cryptocurrency ecosystem and weather market changes by diversifying their investments across many assets. Among the many advantages of diversification are lower risk, more exposure to possibilities, and the possibility of long-term success.

A percentage of your cryptocurrency portfolio should be allocated to well-known cryptocurrencies with a track record of success. Other ways to diversify your holdings include sector-based diversification, sector-based allocation, and keeping up with the most recent developments and trends in the cryptocurrency world. Making wise investing selections and keeping up with the most recent developments in the industry depend on your ability to stay knowledgeable about cryptocurrencies.

Understanding that cryptocurrency values are naturally volatile and may fluctuate significantly over short periods of time is crucial to managing the risks associated with investing in cryptocurrencies with prudence and strategy. Global economic circumstances, market sentiment, regulatory changes, and technology improvements are some of the causes contributing to this volatility.

Establish your goals explicitly before investing in cryptocurrencies and decide whether you want to achieve long-term growth, short-term profits, or both. Your risk management and investing choices will be guided by your well-defined objectives.

Decide on the greatest profit you want to make and the utmost loss you are ready to accept for each investment, then set reasonable profit and loss limitations. These boundaries might lessen the impact of emotional biases and stop rash judgments made while the market is fluctuating.

To limit your exposure to possible losses, make use of risk management instruments like stop-loss orders. In order to reduce your downside risk, a stop-loss order tells the system to automatically sell your assets when they hit a specific price.

Spread out the assets in your bitcoin portfolio to lessen the effect of market turbulence. Invest in a variety of well-known cryptocurrencies, intriguing altcoins, and ventures from many industries, including Web3 infrastructure, NFTs, DeFi, and other initiatives.

Before purchasing any cryptocurrency, do a lot of research on the project. Look over the whitepaper, staff, and community support of the organization. Recognize the project's potential uses, tokenomics, and underlying technology. Be cautious and stay away from using too much leverage, since this may increase profits as well as losses. Leverage increases the danger of suffering significant losses in the event that the market goes against you by amplifying the effect of price fluctuations.

Staying informed and seeking help are essential for keeping up with evolving trends and market changes. To keep up with new trends and changes in the industry, participate in online groups, go to educational seminars, and seek advice from reliable sources.

In summary, diversification is an essential tactic for bitcoin investors to reduce risk and improve their prospects of success in the dynamic market. By using these tactics, investors may lessen the effects of market swings and improve their entire investing strategy by making sure they are knowledgeable on the most recent developments and trends in the bitcoin space.

Investing In Early-Stage Startups

Healthcare, education, and entertainment are just a few of the areas that are changing as a result of emerging trends and businesses. Some of the new businesses that are worth considering for investment include eSports, cleantech, wearables, driverless vehicles, lab-grown meat, commercial space flight, and generative AI. These sectors have the potential to completely transform a number of other industries, including healthcare, education, and entertainment.

Key market trends include the emergence of the digital economy, the transition to a knowledge-based economy, the globalization of markets, the expansion of developing markets, and the aging of the population are also influencing the global economy. Investors may make better investment selections by having a better understanding of these tendencies.

Making wise investment selections requires having a certain level of risk tolerance, particularly for early-stage firms. Because of their potential for failure, limited track record, and untested business strategies, early-stage companies are often regarded as high-risk investments. Take into account your present financial status, your investing objectives, and your attitude toward risk emotionally to ascertain your level of risk tolerance.

When establishing investing objectives, take into account elements including your comfort level with risk, investment horizon, and existing financial status. For instance, you could prefer to invest in lower risk assets if you require short-term returns or have a lengthy investment horizon and are prepared to weather market changes.

The risks and possible benefits of any investment opportunity should be carefully considered while analyzing prospective investments. Furthermore, keeping up with rising market trends and industry developments may assist investors in making better-informed financial choices. In conclusion, in order for investors to make well-informed choices regarding investing in a variety of sectors, they must have a solid grasp of growing industries and market trends. Investors may make well-informed choices that enhance their financial well-being by evaluating risk tolerance, establishing investing objectives, and taking into account variables including emotional stability, financial stability, and risk tolerance.

Because they help match investment options with risk tolerance, investment objectives are essential for making well-informed investment decisions. Financial objectives, a desired timeline, the rate of return, and the quantity required for investments to grow should all be taken into account when creating investment goals. When risk tolerance and investment objectives are in line, one may make well-informed decisions, such as giving early-stage firms with greater returns preference over conservative investments with lower risk profiles.

Managing risk and raising the likelihood of reaching long-term financial objectives need diversification, which is particularly important when investing in early-stage businesses because of their uncertain business concepts, spotty performance histories, and failure probability. Among the many benefits of diversification are lower risk, higher returns, and better sleep. Investors may lessen their risk of a single firm failing by distributing their capital across many companies. This also helps to even out swings and provide more steady profits over time.

It is advisable for early-stage businesses to vary in a number of ways, including industry, stage, region, and business strategy. Investing in startups in a variety of sectors lowers exposure to risks, phases, and geographical areas unique to a certain industry. Investing in startups with diverse business models lowers exposure to the failure of certain techniques or technologies, while investing in startups from different geographies diversifies exposure to various economic contexts and regulatory landscapes.

While distribution is a tried-and-true method of risk management and raising the likelihood of long-term investment success, it is not a guarantee against losses. Before making any investing choices, carefully consider your financial status, investment objectives, and risk tolerance.

Performing due diligence is an essential phase in the investing process, particularly when evaluating firms in their early stages. In order to reduce the risk of failure and make well-informed judgments, it entails investigating and evaluating possible investments. Understanding the business model, assessing the leadership team, examining financial projections, evaluating the market opportunity, reviewing intellectual property (IP), taking legal and regulatory compliance into account, assessing valuation, and obtaining professional and legal advice are all important components of due diligence on early-stage startups.

Due diligence is a constant process, and in order to evaluate their investment choice and make any necessary modifications, investors need keep a close eye on the startup's development, financial performance, and market circumstances. Getting involved in the startup environment may be very beneficial for seasoned and novice investors alike. Investors may access a plethora of information, prospects, and prospective collaborations by immersing themselves in the ecosystem of entrepreneurs, innovators, and other investors.

Participating in startup events, joining online communities and forums, joining startup organizations, following thought leaders and influencers, volunteering time and skills to support accelerators, incubators, or mentorship programs, attending major startup conferences and summits, tuning in to startup podcasts and webinars, establishing connections with universities and entrepreneurship programs, and getting involved with local startup communities are some of the ways to interact with the startup community.

Through active participation in the startup ecosystem, investors may access a multitude of possibilities, insights, and information. Making these relationships and gaining new insights may help them better understand the startup environment, guide their investment choices, and even result in profitable ventures.

,

Doing due diligence is an essential component of the investing process, especially when thinking about early-stage firms. Investors can reduce the risk of failure and make well-informed decisions by studying the business model, assessing the leadership team, examining IP, analyzing financial projections, evaluating market opportunity, taking legal and regulatory compliance into account, and obtaining professional legal advice. Interacting with the startup ecosystem is crucial to the investing process since it may provide insightful information, business alliances, and funding prospects.

It's essential to keep up with the regulatory landscape in your area if you want to make startup investments. It guarantees adherence to the law, safeguarding investors, facilitating the investment process, providing access to rewards and incentives, and minimizing red tape. Take into consideration the following strategies to keep informed:

1. Keep an Eye on Regulatory Bodies: Take the time to visit the websites and publications of relevant regulatory agencies, such industry organizations, securities commissions, and financial regulators. Updates on proposed amendments, revisions to regulations, and compliance requirements may be found in these sources.

2. Seek Legal Counsel: To get customized guidance on relevant legislation, aid with due diligence, and handle complicated legal requirements, get in touch with seasoned legal counsel who specializes in startup investments.

3. Participate in webinars and industry events: Attend seminars, webinars, and events tailored to your sector that are centered on regulatory compliance and startup financing. To obtain frequent information on regulatory developments, legal analyses, and expert comments, subscribe to industry newsletters and publications that are specifically focused on startup investments and regulatory problems.

4. Network with businesses and Startup Investors: Make connections with seasoned local businesses and investors to learn from their experiences and get insight into navigating the regulatory environment.

You may minimize risks, make sure your startup investments comply with legal standards, and increase your chances of success by keeping up with changes in the regulatory landscape.

A precise and well-thought-out exit plan is essential for profitable startup investments. It describes your intended strategy for realizing investment returns and withdrawing from your position. When creating your exit plan, take into account your expectations for the startup's success, your risk tolerance, and your investment objectives. When creating your departure plan, keep the following important stages in mind:

1. Examine Exit Options: Determine if your investment might be exited via a management buyout (MBO), an IPO, or an acquisition by a bigger business. Based on the industry, development stage, and financial performance of the company, evaluate the possibility and viability of each alternative.

2. Establish Timeline Anticipations: Establish a realistic deadline for your departure, taking into account the startup's development trajectory, market trends, and possible exit routes.

3. Establish value objectives: Set value objectives for your exit, evaluating the startup's financial performance, growth prospects, and similar firms in the sector.

4. Keep an eye on market conditions Keep up with advancements in the industry, the macroeconomic environment, and market trends that may affect the startup's value and exit prospects.

5. examine Liquidity Alternatives: If an IPO or acquisition is not imminent, examine alternative liquidity possibilities, such as secondary markets or private equity buyouts, to analyze their terms and conditions and match with your investment objectives.

Optimizing the exit plan is crucial for optimizing the returns on initial investments, offering guidance, supporting informed investment choices, and facilitating a smooth and efficient departure process.

Chapter 3

Common Side Hustle
Investing Mistakes to Avoid

Not diversifying your portfolio

A key concept in investing is diversification, which lowers risk, safeguards cash, and improves long-term financial health. An intolerable amount of risk is exposed to investors by concentrated portfolios, which are highly invested in a single asset class or closely linked assets. These portfolios may be exposed to risks unique to a certain firm or industry, which might cause an excessive dependence on the success of that particular business or industry.

Concentrated portfolios are more vulnerable to market changes because they are more sensitive to general market movements, which may magnify both profits and losses. These kinds of portfolios have the potential to decline at frightening rates during market downturns, forcing investors to deal with significant losses.

Simple asset allocation to complex hedging methods are examples of diversification tactics. Mutual funds, exchange-traded funds (ETFs), or building a portfolio of individual stocks and bonds may all be used to accomplish diversification. An investor's time horizon, investment goals, and risk tolerance all influence the best diversification plan.

To sum up, diversity is crucial for surviving the challenging and sometimes stormy world of investment. Investing in a diverse range of assets, including stocks, bonds, real estate, and commodities, enables investors to mitigate risk, safeguard their wealth, and improve their overall financial prospects over the long haul. Although concentrated portfolios may provide exceptional returns on occasion, the dangers are far greater than the possible gains. Welcome diversity and set off on a path to successful, long-term investing.

A key component of financial planning is diversification, which may be accomplished in a number of ways. Investing in mutual funds or exchange-traded funds (ETFs), which provide quick diversification with a single investment, is one such technique. Purchasing individual stocks and bonds is an additional choice that gives you more control over your money, but it also requires more time and is riskier. To give your money time to grow and to stop worrying about the short-term swings in the market, it is imperative that you invest for the long term and start early.

You may attain your financial objectives, remain invested for the long run, and get a better night's sleep with diversification. This is because, in the event that the value of one investment declines, there is less chance of losing everything. Because diversified portfolios are less susceptible to losses from a single bad investment, they are less likely to experience significant losses from any one asset type.

One of the most frequent mistakes individuals make when investing in side gigs is to overlook diversity. They could invest all of their funds in one thing, such stocks, real estate, or cryptocurrencies, as it can appear like a quick and easy method to become rich. But in reality, this is a highly dangerous tactic. Since it lessens your exposure to any one asset type, diversification helps to lower your risk. In other words, if one of your assets underperforms, you are less likely to lose a significant amount of money.
A well-balanced portfolio may help you reach your financial objectives and enjoy peace of mind, better returns, lower risk, and the flexibility to continue engaged. Because diversified portfolios smooth out market swings, they often beat non-diversified portfolios over the long run.

Investing in a range of asset types, such as equities, bonds, real estate, and commodities, may help diversify your side hustle assets. If you are risk averse, you may devote a larger portion of your portfolio to bonds by allocating your assets based on your risk tolerance; if you are more comfortable with risk, you can assign a larger portion to stocks. As your assets increase, you must also regularly rebalance your portfolio.

Although diversification cannot protect you from losses, it is a crucial strategy for lowering risk and increasing long-term investment returns. You may raise your chances of reaching your financial aims and goals by diversifying your assets in your side business.

Myths about a non-diversified strategy to side hustle investing often cause people to focus all of their money on one particular asset class or even side project, putting their financial goals at danger and exposing them to unnecessary risk. It's critical to comprehend the realities of diversification and build a strong side hustle portfolio in order to debunk these misconceptions and provide side hustlers with a competent investment plan.

The first myth is that diversity reduces returns and hence the possibility of making significant profits. Diversification protects against both the bottoms of catastrophic losses and the peaks of spectacular profits. You may successfully reduce the impact of market swings and industry-specific risks by spreading your holdings across many assets, which will help your portfolio withstand periods of economic volatility.

The second myth is that market timing performs worse than diversification since it's a difficult task that few people can really master. As a solid tactic, diversification serves as a dependable defense against the irrationality of markets. Exchange-traded funds (ETFs) and mutual funds are two easily accessible instruments and techniques that may help accomplish diversification. Diversification may be achieved even when selecting individual stocks and bonds by carefully selecting assets from various sectors and geographical areas.

Establishing your risk tolerance, diversifying your investments across asset classes, investing within asset classes, rebalancing your portfolio on a regular basis, and seeking professional advice if you lack the time or experience to manage your portfolio independently are all strategic steps to building a resilient side hustle portfolio. Recall that the goal of diversity is to manage and mitigate risk rather than completely eliminate it in order to protect your hard-earned wealth. Accepting diversity gives you the ability to create a side hustle portfolio that is sturdy enough to withstand market fluctuations and clear the way for long-term success.

To sum up, diversification helps protect your hard-earned savings by managing and reducing risk rather than completely eliminating it. Accepting diversity gives you the ability to create a side hustle portfolio that is sturdy enough to withstand market fluctuations and clear the way for long-term success.

Investing requires diversification, and this is particularly true for side hustle investments. You may improve your chances of reaching your financial objectives and protect your assets by heeding the practical advice provided above. Investing for the long term and starting early are key. Your money has more time to grow the earlier you start investing, and the longer you invest, the less you have to worry about gyrations in the market.

When it comes to side hustle investing, there is a recurring contradiction that people know how important diversity is, yet they don't always apply it to their own portfolios. This essay explores the psychological underpinnings of this hesitation and highlights the need of implementing a thorough investing plan.

focused investments have a psychological bias that might cause people to ignore the hazards that come with using such a focused strategy. This psychological bias might cause people to ignore the inherent hazards connected with such a focused strategy. It is often motivated by optimism and a trust in one's ability to properly foresee market moves.

People often turn to the comfortable and ostensibly straightforward route of focused investments while navigating the complexity of diversification since it may lead to emotions of overwhelm and uncertainty. Diversification entails a certain amount of control relinquishment, as it acknowledges the important influence of external variables and market forces on investment results. Because of the psychological demand for control that this aspect of uncertainty might elicit, people may be drawn to concentrated investments because they feel like they have more control over their financial future.

Successful side hustle investment management requires a complete approach with diversity as a pillar. Idiosyncratic risks may be efficiently mitigated and portfolio resilience against market changes increased by investing across a number of asset classes, sectors, and geographic areas. Although it seems sense that concentrated assets have a psychological pull, diversifying your portfolio is a wise way to protect your financial health. People may make choices that are in line with their long-term financial objectives by understanding the psychological elements that underlie aversion to diversification and implementing a thorough investing plan.

Finally, diversity is the cornerstone of a wise investing plan, especially in the fast-paced world of side gigs. Through recognition of the difficulties experienced by those who disregard diversity and adoption of the useful guidance provided above, you will enable yourself to make wise choices, protect your assets, and clear the way to reaching your financial goals. Recall that the goal of diversity is to manage and mitigate risk rather than completely eliminate it in order to safeguard your hard-earned wealth. Invest in a range of asset types, including commodities, equities, bonds, and real estate.

Investing Too Much Money In One Area

One of the most important components of investing is diversification, which distributes assets across different asset classes, sectors, and geographic areas in an effort to lower total portfolio risk. You lessen the negative effects of market swings on the value of your portfolio by avoiding placing all of your eggs in one basket. Stocks, bonds, real estate, technology, healthcare, consumer products, and geographic diversification are examples of asset classes that exhibit asset class diversity.

Understanding investment possibilities, sectors, and market trends is critical for effective investing. Investment principles are also necessary. Important aspects in this process include researching various asset classes, comprehending financial jargon, keeping up with economic data, investigating investment choices, being knowledgeable and flexible, and routinely evaluating the asset allocation of your portfolio.

Investing in exchange-traded funds, or ETFs, is a great way for novices to get started in the world of investing. A few benefits of these passive investing alternatives include accessibility, transparency, low expenses, tax efficiency, and diversity. Index funds and exchange-traded funds (ETFs) mimic a particular market index, offering immediate industry and company diversification. They also provide reduced turnover, cheap expenses, openness, and capital gains distributions.

A key component of effective investing is setting realistic financial objectives and matching your investments to your risk tolerance. Establish your investing objectives. These might be long-term (five years or more) objectives, like retirement planning or paying for a child's education, or short-term (less than five years) objectives. Determine your level of risk tolerance, which might range from aggressive to moderate. While moderate portfolios distribute a mix of stocks, bonds, and balanced funds, conservative portfolios have an emphasis on low-risk assets like bonds and stable-value funds. A higher percentage of equities and growth-oriented assets are seen in aggressive portfolios.

Your financial condition and objectives are reflected in your portfolio, which you establish by matching your investments to your goals and risk tolerance. This strategy efficiently manages your risk exposure while maximizing the possibility that you will meet your investing goals.

Recall that if your financial situation and ambitions change over time, so too may your investing goals and risk tolerance. Make sure your portfolio is in line with your present circumstances by reviewing it on a regular basis and making any necessary modifications.

To sum up, diversification is a tried-and-true investing strategy that may greatly improve long-term investment performance and financial stability. Understanding financial basics, investigating investment possibilities, keeping up with industry developments, and routinely evaluating the asset allocation of your portfolio are all necessary for making well-informed selections. You may build a portfolio that matches your financial condition and ambitions by setting realistic investing goals and matching your investments to your risk tolerance. This will maximize the possibility that you will achieve your goals while efficiently limiting risk exposure.

Regardless of the asset's price, a defined amount of money is regularly invested into a certain investment using the dollar-cost averaging (DCA) investment technique. Investors may benefit from this methodical approach in a number of ways, especially while navigating unpredictable market situations. By distributing investments across time and purchasing more shares during periods of low price and less shares during periods of high price, DCA lessens the effects of market volatility. Additionally, it cultivates a disciplined approach to investing, promoting steady investment even in the face of volatile market situations.

DCA invests a set amount at any price, eliminating the emotional roller coaster that comes with attempting to forecast market changes. It is appropriate for novice investors who may not have the knowledge or experience to timing the market well. Because it lessens the danger of investing at a market high and lessens the effect of price fluctuations, DCA is particularly advantageous in unpredictable markets. You may buy additional shares at a discount during downturns, boosting your total ownership and perhaps profiting from future price growth. Because DCA removes the anxiety associated with attempting to forecast market fluctuations, it offers psychological advantages. Consistent investing minimizes decision fatigue and cultivates a feeling of control. In conclusion, DCA is a useful investing approach that offers psychological advantages, encourages disciplined investing practices, and lessens the effects of market volatility.

One of the most important steps you can take to customize your investing path is to speak with a financial counselor. Personalized advice and suggestions based on your particular financial status, objectives, and risk tolerance may be given by them. Their knowledge can guide you through the complexity of investing and assist you in making choices that are consistent with your overall financial strategy.

Getting expert counsel has the following advantages:

1. A customized investment plan: Financial advisers will collaborate closely with you to comprehend your long-term investment objectives, risk tolerance, and financial status. They will create a customized investing strategy that fits your unique goals and requirements.

2. Professional advice and recommendations: Financial advisers provide insights into different asset classes, investment strategies, and market trends since they have a wealth of knowledge and expertise in the investing world. They can help you create a risk management plan that fits your level of risk tolerance.

3. Tax planning and considerations: Financial advisers may help you minimize your tax obligation and maximize your total returns by incorporating tax considerations into your investing strategy.

4. continuous help and portfolio reassessments: A financial adviser will provide continuous support and periodically examine your portfolio to make sure it stays in line with your circumstances as your financial condition and aspirations change.

Recall that frequent evaluation and rebalancing are necessary components of successful investment. You may make sure that your portfolio stays in line with your current financial objectives and market circumstances by routinely evaluating the performance of your portfolio and modifying the allocation according to your investment plan.

Overtrading

Overtrading is a common issue among new traders, as it can have significant negative consequences on their profits in the long run. Key consequences of overtrading include increased transaction costs, emotional trading, neglecting research and analysis, stress and anxiety, and depletion of capital.

To avoid overtrading, traders should develop a trading plan, stick to it, set daily or weekly trading limits, take breaks, and seek professional help. These tips can help avoid the negative consequences of overtrading and increase their chances of success as a trader.

Emotional vulnerability is another psychological challenge faced by novice traders. The allure of quick profits and the fear of missing out (FOMO) can drive beginners to impulsively execute trades without proper analysis or adherence to their trading plan. This emotional reactivity leads to chasing short-term gains at the expense of long-term profitability.

Neglecting due diligence is another significant issue that arises from the relentless pursuit of trades. Overtrading creates a sense of urgency, pushing them to make hasty decisions based on fleeting market movements rather than carefully evaluating a stock's fundamentals and technical indicators. This lack of due diligence increases the likelihood of making poorly informed trades that result in losses.

Stress and anxiety are another significant issue that arises from the constant pressure to make profitable trades and the fear of making mistakes. Overtrading becomes a source of stress and anxiety, affecting a beginner's mental well-being and hindering their ability to make sound trading decisions. Depletion of trading capital is another significant issue that beginners face. The cycle of impulsive trades often leads to a string of losses, eroding their financial capacity to continue trading. This demoralizing experience discourages them from pursuing their trading goals.

Impedated learning and growth is another significant challenge faced by beginners. The constant cycle of trades prevents them from taking the time to reflect on their actions, identify recurring patterns, and refine their approach. This stagnation impedes their growth as traders and limits their chances of achieving long-term success.

To effectively combat the psychological pitfalls of overtrading, beginners can adopt several strategies:

1. cultivate patience and discipline:

Patience and discipline are cornerstones of successful trading. Beginners should approach trading with a long-term mindset, avoiding the temptation to chase immediate gains. By adhering to a well-defined trading plan and avoiding impulsive decisions, they can maintain control over their trading actions.

2. embrace thorough research and analysis:
Before executing any trade, beginners should conduct thorough research and analysis, meticulously evaluating a stock's fundamentals, technical indicators, and overall market conditions. This due diligence will provide a solid foundation for making informed trading decisions.

3. manage emotions effectively:
Emotions can be powerful influencers in trading, but beginners should learn to manage them effectively. Employing relaxation techniques, taking breaks from trading, and seeking guidance from experienced traders can help maintain emotional composure and make rational decisions.

4. establish realistic trading goals:
Setting realistic goals aligned with risk tolerance and experience level can help beginners manage expectations and

avoid the pressure of making quick profits. By focusing on steady, consistent growth, beginners can develop a sustainable trading approach.

By overcoming the psychological pitfalls of overtrading and adopting these strategies, beginners can set themselves on a path toward successful trading, navigating the markets with a disciplined, patient, and well-informed approach. Overtrading is a common trading habit that can hinder a beginner's decision-making process and lead to significant losses. It is crucial for beginners to recognize the signs of overtrading and adopt a more disciplined approach.

Excessive trading frequency is a strong indicator of overtrading, as it often stems from the pursuit of quick profits without considering thorough analysis and a well-defined trading plan. Overtraders often fall prey to the temptation of chasing market movements, impulsively entering and exiting trades based on short-term price movements. This reactive approach overlooks the significance of fundamentals and technical indicators, leading to poorly informed decisions.

Ignoring a trading plan is another sign of overtrading, as it serves as a roadmap for making disciplined trading decisions. Emotional trading is a hallmark of overtrading, as beginners succumb to fear, greed, and impatience, making impulsive decisions driven by emotions rather than sound analysis. This emotional reactivity often leads to poor trading outcomes.

Neglecting risk management is another sign of overtrading, as failure to set stop-loss orders and adhere to position sizing rules exposes beginners to excessive risk, amplifying the potential for significant losses. To combat overtrading and adopt a more disciplined approach, beginners can implement the following strategies:

1. Develop a Structured Trading Plan: A well-defined trading plan provides a framework for making informed decisions. It should outline entry and exit criteria, risk management strategies, and overall trading objectives. Adhering to this plan instills discipline and prevents impulsive trading.

2. Prioritize Thorough Analysis: Before executing any trade, beginners should conduct thorough research and analysis. Evaluating a stock's fundamentals, technical indicators, and overall market conditions provides a solid foundation for making informed decisions.

3. Seek Continuous Learning: Trading is a continuous learning process, and beginners should embrace opportunities to expand their knowledge and refine their skills. Setting realistic trading goals aligned with their risk tolerance and experience level can help beginners manage expectations and avoid the pressure of making quick profits.

4. Manage Emotions Effectively: Emotions can be powerful influencers in trading, but beginners should learn to manage them effectively. Employing relaxation techniques, taking breaks from trading, and seeking guidance from experienced traders can help maintain emotional composure and make rational decisions.

By recognizing the signs of overtrading and implementing these strategies, beginners can cultivate a more disciplined and effective trading approach, setting themselves on a path toward success in the trading world.

Impatience is a common issue that can have significant negative impacts on a beginner's investment portfolio. It often leads to unrealistic expectations of quick profits, leading to impulsive trading decisions without proper analysis or adherence to a trading plan. This rush to make money often results in frequent trades based on short-term market fluctuations or emotional reactions, rather than a sound understanding of fundamentals and risk management.

The detrimental effects of impatience on a beginner's investment portfolio are multifaceted. Overtrading generates excessive transaction costs due to frequent commissions and fees, which gradually eat into profits. Impulsive trades without thorough analysis often lead to poor trading decisions, increasing the likelihood of losses that further erode profits.

Impatience fosters an environment where emotions dictate trading decisions, overriding rational judgment. The fear of missing out (FOMO) and the allure of quick gains can drive beginners to chase market movements without proper risk assessment, leading to impulsive trades that often result in losses.

Neglecting due diligence is another detrimental effect of impatience. The relentless pursuit of trades often forces beginners to overlook the crucial step of thorough research and analysis. This lack of due diligence increases the likelihood of making poorly informed trades that result in losses.

Stress and anxiety are another significant impact of impatience-driven overtrading. The constant pressure to make profitable trades and the fear of making mistakes can take a significant toll on a beginner's mental well-being, affecting their overall health and emotional balance. This emotional turmoil further clouds their judgment and hinders their ability to make sound trading decisions.

Overtrading can rapidly deplete a beginner's trading capital, leaving them with limited resources to capitalize on future opportunities. The cycle of impulsive trades often leads to a string of losses, eroding their financial capacity to continue trading. This demoralizing experience can discourage them from pursuing their trading goals.

To combat the detrimental effects of impatience on their investment portfolios, beginners should cultivate patience and adopt a disciplined trading approach. Establishing realistic expectations, developing a trading plan, seeking thorough analysis, managing emotions effectively, and seeking continuous learning are essential steps to avoid the pitfalls of overtrading and embark on a more successful trading journey.

To combat overtrading and achieve trading goals, beginners should adopt several strategies. These include setting realistic and specific goals that align with their risk tolerance, experience level, and financial situation. A well-defined trading plan is essential for making informed decisions and adhering to a disciplined approach. Thorough research and analysis are also crucial before executing any trades, as it provides a solid foundation for making rational decisions.

Practicing patience and discipline is essential for successful trading, as beginners should avoid the temptation to rush into trades and maintain a long-term mindset. Regularly monitoring progress towards trading goals is crucial for evaluating effectiveness and making necessary adjustments.

By setting clear trading goals, adopting a disciplined approach, and managing emotions effectively, beginners can navigate the financial markets with a clear direction, avoiding the pitfalls of overtrading and increasing their likelihood of achieving their long-term investment aspirations. Overtrading, characterized by excessive trading activity, can significantly hinder a beginner's ability to achieve their trading goals and poses a substantial risk to their capital. By adhering to sound risk management principles, beginners can effectively prevent overtrading and safeguard their financial resources.

Establishing a trading plan, setting position sizing limits, using stop-loss orders, maintaining diversification, avoiding revenge trading, taking regular breaks from trading, seeking guidance from experienced traders, continuing learning and improvement, managing emotions effectively, and adhering to risk tolerance are some of the strategies that beginners can follow to cultivate a disciplined trading approach, avoid the pitfalls of overtrading, and safeguard their capital while pursuing their investment goals.

Not Having A Plan

Investment in side projects without a clear financial strategy may have a number of detrimental effects, such as impulsive spending, an uneven distribution of assets, the disregard of financial objectives, emotional investment, and a lack of transparency. Missed chances, inadequate research, and an imbalanced portfolio that exposes investors to undue risk or possible growth prospects are some of the possible outcomes of these possible consequences.

A financial plan acts as a compass, directing investment choices in the direction of a diverse portfolio in line with time horizons and risk tolerance. Investors who don't follow this advice risk having an imbalanced portfolio, which makes them more susceptible to market swings and raises the possibility of suffering substantial losses. Furthermore, investing without a plan often results in a disorganized strategy that overlooks major financial objectives and goals including emergency savings, debt reduction, and retirement savings. Long-term stability and financial security may be compromised by this.

Emotional investing may result in impulsive selling during market downturns or pursuing unrealistic returns in speculative investments, which increases the danger of large losses. Emotional investing can be motivated by fear, greed, or market hype. By using risk management techniques and discipline, a financial plan keeps emotions out of the decision-making process while making investments. Another possible problem with side hustle investing without well-defined and precise investment objectives is a lack of direction and clarity. Without clear goals, it's hard to figure out what the side gig profits are supposed to be used for, which may result in impulsive investing choices that don't always match the person's overall financial goals. It is difficult to track progress, assess performance, and decide how best to allocate and rebalance investments due to this lack of guidance.

Lack of clear investing objectives may also lead to unbalanced asset allocation and financial fragility. Investors risk losing out on possible growth opportunities or ending up with an imbalanced portfolio without these standards, which exposes them to undue risk. Investors who have an imbalanced portfolio are more susceptible to market swings and have a higher risk of suffering large losses.
A careless approach that disregards overall financial considerations might result from neglecting financial goals and priorities. Neglecting crucial components like

emergency reserves, debt repayment, and retirement savings puts long-term stability and financial security at risk.

In conclusion, one's journey to long-term financial success might be derailed by side hustle investing if they neglect to set clear investment objectives. Financial growth may be impeded and significant losses can be increased by impulsive investment, inappropriate asset allocation, emotional investing, lack of direction, and disregard of financial goals. Accepting certain investing objectives offers a clear path for maximizing side gig income, coordinating it with overall financial goals, and guaranteeing reliable, long-term financial plans.

There might be serious financial repercussions if an emergency fund is not established for side business ventures, especially when there are market downturns. An emergency fund is an essential safety net that keeps people from depleting their savings in times of financial hardship and acts as a buffer against unforeseen costs. Insufficient emergency funds may lead to forced asset sales, elevated risk in investments, emotional investing, compromised financial stability, and heightened financial susceptibility.

For side hustle investments to be successful, budgeting is essential. It encourages budgeting, guarantees prudent spending, ranks important responsibilities first, and synchronizes side gig income with long-term financial objectives. If you skip this important step, you run the risk of spending too much and becoming financially vulnerable, forgetting important financial responsibilities, investing goals and stability being hijacked, not having enough financial awareness and control, becoming demoralized and less motivated, and even losing sight of the whole point of starting side businesses.

When investing in a side business, skipping research may have a number of negative effects, the most serious of which being making poor selections that can cost a lot of money. This ignorance may result in irrational expectations, bad choices, and a higher risk of experiencing financial losses.

Another major problem that might lead to investing in a side business with little market potential or facing fierce rivalry is an inadequate evaluation of the market's demand and competitiveness, which can impede profitability and raise the risk of failure. Financial pressure and cash flow issues may also result from underestimating initial start-up costs and continuing expenditures, such as those related to inventory, marketing, or equipment, as well as continuous operations costs like rent, utilities, or supplies.

Ignoring licensing and regulatory compliance requirements may result in penalties, legal problems, and even company closures. Furthermore, side gig options may draw in dishonest or unviable company models, which might result in lost investments and legal troubles.

To sum up, starting a side business without doing extensive study is like sailing into unknown seas without a map or compass. It exposes people to a wide range of dangers, most notably the possibility of making poor judgments that may lead to large financial losses. In-depth research increases the likelihood of a side hustle succeeding and protects financial well-being by offering the information needed to make wise decisions, determine market feasibility, weigh risks, and spot genuine possibilities.

A person's side hustle investment plan may be neglected, which may result in lost opportunities, decreased profitability, higher financial risks, and a disconnection from changing financial objectives. To make sure that side hustle investments are in line with market circumstances, individual financial goals, and the always shifting financial environment, it is essential to adopt a flexible and dynamic strategy.

Since market circumstances are always changing and bringing with them new chances as well as difficulties, a stagnant investing approach may lead to lost opportunities and unrealized growth potential. Additionally, it may cause a departure from financial objectives and goals, which are subject to change over time due to a variety of reasons including life stage, changes in income, and unforeseen costs. Individuals may evaluate and manage these risks via regular evaluations by reallocating assets, using risk mitigation techniques, or changing their entire investing strategy.

Failing to Adjust to Changing Industry Trends and Regulations:
Side hustle investments may be severely impacted by changing industry trends and regulations, which might lead to compliance problems, lower profitability, or obsolescence. Furthermore, a stagnation of investing expertise and knowledge With the emergence of new investment vehicles, strategies, and technology, the financial environment is continuously changing. Frequent reviews provide the chance to remain abreast of these developments, broaden one's understanding of investing, and hone one's investment strategy in order to maximize returns and efficiently manage risks.

When it comes to side hustle investing, one of the most common mistakes people make is not diversifying their investments, which may put them at danger and make their overall performance in the market worse. Spreading assets over several asset classes, sectors, and geographical areas is known as diversification, and it is a fundamental component of successful investing strategies. This helps to reduce the impact of unfavorable market changes. Ignoring this concept may result in a concentration of wealth in one asset or industry, which can increase the impact of adverse market fluctuations and impede long-term financial benefits.

Because the value of an undiversified side hustle portfolio might collapse in the event that the selected asset or sector undergoes a downturn, it can also expose investors to excessive market volatility and speculative risks. Through the process of weighing possible rewards against risk, diversification helps to align investments with long-term goals, promote sustainable development, and reduce the chance of a market-related derailment.

Investing in a side venture without diversifying is like building a home on shaky ground without supporting foundations. People that invest in it run the danger of experiencing increased risks, market volatility, downturns in certain industries, lost opportunities, and emotional traps. By reducing risks, increasing possibilities for development, and ensuring the accomplishment of long-term financial objectives, embracing diversity fortifies the financial framework.

Chapter 4

Case Studies of Successful Side Hustle Investors

Thomas Edison

The phonograph, motion picture camera, and incandescent light bulb are just a few of the ground-breaking technologies that made American icon and renowned inventor Thomas Edison famous. But his inventiveness went beyond these creations; throughout his lifetime, he engaged in a number of business endeavors.

Edison showed an early knack for commerce and experimentation as a young boy, selling newspapers on trains, experimenting with chemicals in his parents' basement, and erecting a temporary laboratory in the cellar. These first pursuits demonstrated his entrepreneurship spirit and established the groundwork for his subsequent undertakings.

When he was younger, Edison took on a number of business ventures that improved his abilities and helped him become wealthy. The speed and effectiveness of telegraph transmission were greatly increased by the automated telegraph repeater he created and commercialized. He also started a manufacturing business that produced carbon telephones and electric pens, both of which were successful in the marketplace.

Edison's business endeavors included a wide range of sectors in addition to innovations. In addition to starting a company that made and marketed phonograph records, he also made investments in the mining sector, going into businesses that manufactured portland cement and iron ore. Even if not all of these endeavors were as profitable as others, they still showed Edison's readiness to take chances and look for novel prospects.

Edison had the means to pursue his more ambitious innovations because to the money he made from his business endeavors. He was able to invest in research and development facilities, engage competent helpers, and carry out extensive experiments thanks to the money he made from his early projects, which included the electric pen and automated telegraph repeater. Edison's journey to ground-breaking innovations would have been much more difficult in the absence of these financial resources.

Edison's less well-known business endeavors were vital in determining his overall success, even though they were sometimes eclipsed by his ground-breaking innovations. They gave him access to capital, priceless expertise, and a comprehensive grasp of the business sector. By following his entrepreneurial instincts and being open to new chances, he was able to achieve amazing success in a variety of sectors, solidifying his reputation as one of the most influential and productive people in American history.

In addition to being a prolific inventor and national treasure, Thomas Edison was a brilliant businessman who accumulated significant money by making a number of astute investments. Beyond his ground-breaking innovations, he was an entrepreneur who explored a wide variety of side projects that were crucial to his financial success.

One significant venture he made was starting a company that made and marketed phonograph recordings. This enabled him to combine his creative and commercial acumen while also taking advantage of the phonograph's increasing popularity. Apart from his engagement in the entertainment sector, Edison also ventured into the mining business, making investments in projects like the manufacturing of portland cement and iron ore mining. These investments showed Edison's wide variety of interests and his willingness to take calculated risks in the hope of making money, even if not all of them were equally successful.

A number of crucial tactical choices contributed to Edison's success in handling his side business investments:

1. Alignment with skills and Interests: To ensure that he could actively contribute to the growth and success of these initiatives, Edison made sure that his investments were carefully chosen to match his skills and interests. Using this strategy, he was able to get the most out of every investment and make the most of his expertise and enthusiasm.

2. Portfolio diversity: Edison understood the value of portfolio diversity in reducing risk and maximizing possible profits. He expanded his chances of success by investing in a variety of sectors, such as mining, entertainment, and communication technology, which lessened his exposure to market swings.

3. Calculated Risk-Taking: Edison never shied away from taking calculated chances because he knew that sometimes exploring new ground could yield big rewards. However, he always approached these investments cautiously, making sure that the possible rewards outweighed the possible risks.

4. Strategic Financial Management: Edison cleverly reinvested a significant amount of the money he made from his side business ventures back into his R&D projects. He

was able to consistently develop and spur his ground-breaking ideas because to this calculated strategy.

Thomas Edison's side business ventures were well-thought-out endeavors that enhanced his creative flair and helped him achieve extraordinary financial achievement rather than serving as a diversion from his creative endeavors. In addition to being a prolific inventor, Edison also proved to be a cunning businessman by diversifying his investment portfolio, matching his investments to his areas of expertise and passion, taking measured risks, and engaging in strategic financial management. These actions cemented Edison's reputation as a true Renaissance man.

Not only was Thomas Edison a well-known American inventor and prolific inventor, but he was also renowned for his exceptional business sense. His significant innovations, which include the phonograph and the incandescent light bulb, have appropriately solidified his historical legacy. But Edison's achievements went beyond these well-known products. He made several side venture investments during his life, some of which were less well-known but yet had a significant impact on his total success.

The automated telegraph repeater, which Edison developed in 1874, changed communication by automatically renewing telegraph signals so they could travel further distances without deteriorating. Thanks to his profitable and extremely successful investment in this revolutionary technology, Edison was able to further extend his research and development endeavors. Edison's purchase of the automated telegraph repeater serves as a reminder to contemporary investors of the significance of:

1. Determining Market Needs: Edison took advantage of a technical development that met the need for better communication infrastructure by identifying it.
2. Recognizing Market Trends: He wisely decided to invest in repeater technology after seeing the rising need for telegraphy that is quicker and more dependable.
3. Capitalizing on Innovation: Edison was an innovator who saw that the telegraph repeater had the potential to revolutionize communication and bring about large financial rewards.

Edison's investment in carbon telephones and electric pens emphasizes the significance of the following for current investors:

1. Early Adoption: To take advantage of the first-mover advantage, Edison made early investments in developing technologies after seeing their potential.

2. Market Focus: He made his goods customer-focused by understanding the rising need for better communication devices.

3. Diversification: To lower risk and increase his sources of income, Edison diversified his investments outside his main innovations.

Thomas Edison's early acceptance of developing technologies, market focus, diversification, and investments in side projects all demonstrated his entrepreneurial attitude. His inventive enthusiasm and openness to new ideas encouraged him to go into a variety of sectors, including the manufacturing of Portland cement and phonograph recordings, in addition to innovations. Aspiring investors may learn a lot from these side projects about the value of diversifying assets, taking a calculated approach to wealth creation, seeing and seizing on new trends, and carrying out extensive due research. We may learn important lessons from Edison's entrepreneurial spirit and unearth useful advice for contemporary investors by looking closely at some of his profitable side venture ventures.

Prolific inventor and national hero Thomas Edison is credited with creating several ground-breaking devices, including the motion picture camera, phonograph, and incandescent lightbulb. But his inventiveness went well beyond these well-known works of art; throughout his lifetime, he attempted a number of business endeavors. His financial portfolio was more than simply a list of assets; it was evidence of his business sense and capacity to see and seize a variety of chances. His side ventures, which included the development of the telegraph, phonograph records, and even the manufacturing of portland cement, brought him significant riches and gave him insightful knowledge of a variety of markets and sectors.

The invention and commercialization of the automated telegraph repeater, which transformed communication by automatically renewing telegraph signals and enabling them to travel larger distances without deterioration, was one of Edison's most profitable side projects. His financial resources to further his R&D and explore even more ambitious discoveries were made possible by this very profitable investment. Important takeaways from the investment in automatic telegraph repeaters include:

1. Determine the demands of the market: Edison took advantage of a technical innovation that met the need for better communication infrastructure, seeing that there was a need.

2. Recognize market trends: When deciding whether to invest in repeater technology, Edison considered the increasing need for telegraphy that was more dependable and quicker.

3. Take advantage of innovation: Edison was a proponent of innovation and saw that the telegraph repeater had the potential to revolutionize communication and bring about large financial rewards.

2. Profit from developing technologies: Edison took use of the first-mover advantage by making early investments in carbon telephones and electric pens.

3. Market focus: Edison made adjustments to his goods to better suit the demands of his customers, seeing the increasing need for better communication devices.

4. Diversification: To lower risk and increase his sources of income, Edison added investments to his portfolio outside of his main innovations.

Edison ventured beyond innovations and into a variety of sectors thanks to his entrepreneurial energy and openness to new chances. His side business ventures, which included the carbon telephones, electric pens, and automated telegraph repeater, showed that he could recognize market demands, capitalize on new technology, diversify his assets, and take measured risks in the hope of making money. Through judicious venture selection that matched his skills and passions, Edison was able to attain extraordinary financial success, cementing his reputation as a Renaissance man.

Jane Doe: How she turned her passion for blogging into a profitable investment

The story of Jane Doe, who started out as a passionate blogger and eventually became a successful businesswoman, is one of perseverance, hard work, and never giving up. Since launching "Jane's Fashion Journal" in 2010, she has gained a devoted readership who value her frank and approachable writing style. As her blog gained popularity, she started looking at methods to make money off of her interest. She tried selling blog advertising, making her own brand of accessories, and even founding an online store.

Along the road, Jane encountered several difficulties, such as rivalry from other blogs and shops and the dynamic fashion industry. She never gave up on her ambition, however. Jane's experience offers valuable lessons about pursuing your passion, having patience, being adaptable, and never giving up.

In order to become a successful businesswoman, Jane Doe has to have perseverance, pursue her passion, be flexible, and never give up. Aspiring business owners may draw inspiration from her experience, which shows that with perseverance, hard work, and devotion, it is possible to transform your passion into a successful company.

Her main takeaways from the experience include figuring out her specialty and audience, building a devoted following, making the most of social media, investigating other revenue streams, creating her own goods, and starting an online store. Jane Doe was able to establish a lucrative and successful company that connected with her audience and helped her cultivate a devoted readership by adhering to these guidelines.

Jane Doe's transformation from an enthusiastic blogger to a successful businesswoman is proof of the value of drive, perseverance, hard effort, and a never-give-up mentality. Jane Doe has effectively converted her passion into a successful business by pursuing her hobbies, using the power of social media, investigating different monetization options, and following her enthusiasm.

Jane Doe's inspirational story of passion, skill, and monetization mastery tells the story of her transformation from a personal finance lover to a profitable financial blogger. Her ability to grow her blog into a successful company is an inspiration to anybody hoping to use their writing and financial acumen to become financially independent.

Jane Doe's success is a result of her in-depth knowledge of her specialty, personal finance. She developed her proficiency in a range of financial subjects, allowing her to provide her readers reliable and insightful commentary. A vast variety of personal financial subjects, from investing and debt management to budgeting and saving, were covered in a consistent and excellent manner. Her writing was excellent, simple to read, and full of helpful suggestions.

Developing authority and trust was essential to building a devoted fan base and drawing in sponsorship offers. She used a variety of monetization techniques, including sponsored articles, affiliate marketing, and collaborations with financial institutions, to diversify her sources of revenue. By producing useful digital goods like e-books, webinars, and online courses, she broadened her product line and gave her readers access to in-depth financial information and resources.

By interacting with her audience in a proactive manner, Jane Doe developed a strong feeling of community. She connected with a larger audience and promoted her blog by using social media channels carefully.

To succeed in the ever-changing financial scene, she had to embrace constant learning and development. She took online classes, went to business events, and kept up with the most recent financial developments.

She succeeded because she never wavered in her zeal and genuineness. Her continuing popularity may be attributed to her ability to stay true to herself and establish a personal connection with her readers.

Finally, Jane Doe's path from a fan of personal finance to a prosperous financial blogger provides insightful insights for anybody hoping to use their writing and financial expertise to become financially independent.

Jane Doe's transformation from an aspiring blogger to a seasoned financial commentator is evidence of her flexibility, tenacity, and keen awareness of the blogging community. Her ability to take advantage of new possibilities and maneuver through the constantly shifting dynamics of the internet world has made her blog a profitable and intellectually stimulating venture.

1. Seeing Obstacles as Chances for Improvement

Jane Doe never back down from a challenge; rather, she saw them as chances for development and improvement. She saw that constant innovation and adaptation were necessary due to the competitive nature of the blogging community. She was able to face challenges head-on and come out stronger because of this mentality.

2. Making the Most of Changing Trends:

Jane Doe continued to be at the forefront of new developments in the blogging community. She aggressively investigated new social media sites, technology, and content formats to raise the profile and interaction of her blog. Her blog was current and attractive to a larger readership because of her innovative approach.

3. Establishing a Group of Faithful Readers:

Jane Doe made her readers feel very much a part of a community. Through conversations, comments, and social media exchanges, she actively engaged with them, building a devoted following that valued her knowledge and wisdom.

4. Changing Up Your Revenue Sources:

In order to ensure the long-term viability of her blog, Jane Doe realized how important it was to diversify her sources of revenue. She experimented with sponsored postings, product endorsements, and even the creation of her own digital goods, going beyond conventional advertising and affiliate marketing. This diversification guaranteed a consistent flow of income while reducing risks.

5. Preserving Credibility and Authenticity:

Jane Doe never wavered in her integrity or reliability. Her voice and ideals never wavered, and she continued to provide objective, well thought-out financial counsel. Her status as a reliable financial expert was further cemented when her readers respected and trusted her for her persistent dedication to ethics.

6. Finding a Happy Medium Between Business and Passion:

Jane Doe was able to strike a balance between her love of personal finance and the commercial side of blogging. She was aware that prudent financial management, strong marketing, and strategic planning were necessary for a blog to be successful.

7. Acknowledging the Strength of Teamwork:

Jane Doe saw the advantages of working together and interacting with other financial bloggers and business professionals. By participating in collaborative webinars, cross-promotion, and guest blogging, she was able to reach a wider audience.

8. Fostering an Attitude of Growth:

Jane Doe developed a development mindset by actively looking for chances to advance her knowledge and skills. She signed up for online courses, went to business conventions, and interacted with mentors.

Jane Doe's transformation from an enthusiastic blogger to a prosperous businesswoman is proof of the strength of ingenuity, tenacity, and strategic thinking.
The inspirational story of Jane Doe's transformation from an enthusiastic blogger to a prosperous businesswoman is one of perseverance, imagination, and astute decision-making. Her ability to turn her blog into a profitable venture offers hope to budding content producers and bloggers everywhere.

Jane Doe's adventure started with her sincere passion for blogging, and she discovered great satisfaction in imparting her knowledge, insights, and experiences to the world. Her will to achieve was strengthened by her desire, despite obstacles. She understood how crucial it was to identify her specialty and modify her writing to appeal to a certain target market. She was able to draw in a devoted following who really appreciated her views thanks to her calculated strategy. Jane Doe did more than just write blog entries. She participated in conversations, left thoughtful comments, and developed sincere relationships with her readers. Her readers felt more a part of the community and her blog became a focus for conversation as a result of her community-building strategy.

As her blog grew in popularity, Jane Doe looked into several ways to make money off of her interest. She tried her hand at sponsored articles, affiliate marketing, and even making her own digital goods. Her financial security was ensured by the diversity of her sources of income, which freed her up to concentrate on producing top-notch content.

Jane Doe persisted in her dedication to lifelong learning and flexibility. She took online classes, went to industry events, and kept up with the newest developments in social media, blogging, and marketing. Because of her flexibility, her blog was able to stay competitive and current in the rapidly evolving digital landscape.

Jane Doe's accomplishment was a clear example of the effectiveness of networking and social media. She made good use of social media sites to reach a larger audience and increase her reach. Her social media presence increased the exposure of her site and brought in new followers.

Jane Doe's trip was not without difficulties. She had to contend with obstacles, rivalry, and dynamic algorithms. She never quit, however. Her success was largely attributed to her endurance, patience, and unshakeable faith in her own skills.

Motivating people with her accomplishments:

Start by writing about something you really love and appreciate if you want to follow Jane Doe's route. Your work will be infused with passion, drawing in devoted readers.

Identify your target market and niche:
Recognize your target audience and adapt your work to suit their requirements and interests. You'll be able to establish a solid rapport with your audience by doing this.

Interact with your audience:
By answering questions, joining conversations, and connecting with your followers on social media, you may create a community.

Investigate your choices for monetization: Experiment with various monetization techniques, such affiliate marketing, sponsored articles, and producing your own digital goods, to diversify your sources of revenue.

Never stop learning: Keep up with the most recent developments in social media, blogging, and marketing. Maintaining a competitive and up-to-date blog requires constant learning.

It takes time and work to create a successful blog, so be persistent and patient. Don't let failures depress you. Continue producing top-notch content while keeping your long-term objectives in mind.

Recall:

The path of Jane Doe is proof of the strength of commitment, passion, and foresight. Anyone can transform their blogging ideas into a profitable venture with a little effort, persistence, and adaptability.

Henry Ford

With his revolutionary assembly line manufacturing technique and the classic Model T vehicle, Henry Ford, the renowned automotive pioneer, transformed the automotive industry. But there were obstacles in his way of accomplishment. Before founding the Ford Motor Company, Henry Ford Company, and Detroit Automobile Company, Ford had two early failures. These first endeavors taught him important insights that influenced his attitude to business and production.

Ford's first venture into automobile manufacture was the Detroit Automobile Company, established in 1899. But his insistence on perfection and preference for design over productivity caused delays and strained relations with investors. Disagreements between Ford and his financial backers—who were eager to see results—caused the firm to collapse in 1901. Undeterred, Ford joined up with the same backers to establish the Henry Ford Company in 1901, but his fixation on perfecting the design of his car, the Model A, presented further difficulties for this business endeavor. Impatient investors forced Ford out of the business in 1902.

Ford learned important lessons from these early setbacks that would prove critical to his success later on: keep a strict budget, emphasize manufacturing efficiency, and adjust to client requests. Ford founded the Ford Motor Company in 1903 and unveiled the ground-breaking Model T in 1908 with these lessons in mind.

Important components of Ford's ground-breaking mass manufacturing strategy changed the way cars were made, lowering their cost and increasing their accessibility to a larger group of buyers. Ford's assembly line technique, which divided the assembly process into a number of little, specialized jobs that could be completed by less-skilled people, replaced the ineffective craft manufacturing approach. Greater specialization and efficiency were made possible by this division of labor, which also markedly decreased manufacturing costs and times.

The moving assembly line, which removed the need for workers to go around the automobile and instead brought the car to them as it moved down a conveyor belt, was a key component of Ford's mass production strategy. This constant motion improved productivity and significantly simplified the assembling procedure.

Ford made his car parts interchangeable by standardizing them in order to achieve mass manufacturing. Further cutting manufacturing costs, this uniformity minimized the need for custom-made components and streamlined the assembly process.

Additionally, Ford sought vertical integration, which gave them command over a number of production-related activities, such as locating raw materials, producing components, and distributing them. Ford was able to significantly cut manufacturing costs and guarantee a consistent supply of materials thanks to this method, which also offered him more control over the pricing and quality of components.

Ford's investment strategies—which included building new technologies, seeking vertical integration, sponsoring the development of manufacturing facilities, and reinvesting a significant amount of his earnings back into the company—were a major factor in his success. In order to diversify his income sources and lessen his dependency on a single commodity, he also made forays into other industries, such as the manufacture of glass and tractors.

Henry Ford's management approach had a significant effect on the Ford Motor Company's success and still has an impact on corporate executives today. His creative manufacturing methods, along with his clear vision and uncompromising dedication to quality, revolutionized the automotive sector and helped Ford Motor Company rise to prominence on a worldwide scale.

Henry Ford's management approach may teach us a lot about how to run businesses and investments. He personified a clear vision, gave workers the freedom to own their job, placed a high priority on efficiency and production, cared about the well-being of his staff, and constantly innovated to remain one step ahead of the competition. Beyond the automotive sector, Ford's legacy offers guidance on efficient management and leadership techniques. The contemporary corporate world was defined by his inventive attitude, which he combined with his dedication to employee welfare and continual development to turn Ford Motor Company into a worldwide powerhouse.

The extraordinary success of the Ford Motor Company was largely attributed to Ford's extraordinary ability to predict market needs and modify his investment methods appropriately. This solidified Ford's status as one of the most significant personalities in business history. His capacity to recognize new trends, comprehend customer preferences, and modify his investment strategy appropriately provides insightful guidance for securing one's financial endeavors for the future.

Ford's flexibility and vision provide insightful advice on how to make one's financial endeavors future-proof. Create a strategic vision for your company or investment by focusing on the future with clarity and forward thinking. Put a strong emphasis on consumer insights and market research. To understand how your target market is changing and what it wants, you should constantly collect data, examine consumer behavior, and spot new trends. Retain agility and flexibility: Be ready to modify your product offerings and investment plans in response to shifting customer preferences, market circumstances, and technology breakthroughs.

Accept innovation and continuous improvement: Look for new methods, tools, and techniques all the time to better your goods and services and maintain your competitive edge in the ever changing business environment. To guarantee the long-term sustainability of your investing initiatives, cultivate financial discipline and prudence by adhering to basic financial management techniques, keeping a solid balance sheet, and refraining from taking on excessive risk.

Henry Ford has shown unrelenting tenacity via his incredible journey from a teenage inventor to one of the most powerful leaders in corporate history. His success as an investor was largely attributed to his unrelenting faith in his vision and capacity for learning from mistakes.

Early in life, Ferdinand Ford showed signs of an enterprising spirit when his first automobile company, the Detroit Automobile Company, failed in 1901. But after reflecting on his errors, he redirected his energies and founded the Henry Ford Company in 1903. Ford persisted in his goal of bringing cars into the reach of the general public, unfazed by these obstacles. In 1903, with the financial support of other investors, he established the Ford Motor Company. Henry Ford's resilience in the face of obstacles led to his success as an investor. Throughout his path, he shown resilience, learned from mistakes, and unflinching faith in his goal of enabling the general public to own vehicles. Ford's ability to reflect on his failures, pinpoint areas for improvement, and use these learnings to guide his future initiatives demonstrated his tenacity and flexibility.

Beyond the car business, Ford has left a lasting legacy that may teach budding investors a lot. He never lost sight of his goals, accepted resilience, continued to be adaptable, and learnt from his failures. His mass manufacturing methods and creative business plans revolutionized the automobile sector, lowering the cost of automobiles and increasing their accessibility while influencing contemporary capitalism and corporate social responsibility.

Ford's investment choices had an influence on society in a number of ways, including the creation of jobs, economic expansion, personal freedom and mobility, cultural change, industrialization and supply chain development, mass consumption and consumerism, and the early 20th century economic boom. The lives of his workers were much enhanced by his high $5 daily salary, which also increased demand for products and services and stimulated the economy. Ford's methods of mass manufacturing also opened up a new consumer market, which increased demand for products and services in a number of other sectors.

Ultimately, Ford's prosperity boosted output, employment, and consumption during the early 20th century economic boom. His attempts to expand internationally, especially in Europe, sparked economic cooperation and globalization.

Lessons on ethical business practices and corporate social responsibility may also be learned from Ferdinand's legacy.

He gave an example of how companies may succeed financially and yet improve society. In addition to improving productivity and brand reputation, fair labor standards, employee empowerment, and community involvement may have a good social effect. It is the duty of businesses to use resources sensibly and to operate in a sustainable manner, safeguarding the environment. Sustainable business practices are shown by Ford's initiatives to promote cleaner technology, improve manufacturing processes, and decrease waste.

Finally, Ford's financial choices illustrated the effectiveness of corporate social responsibility. Ford demonstrates the power of corporate social responsibility via its charitable undertakings, like the Ford Foundation, which support education, infrastructure, and social welfare projects while investing in local communities.

In summary, Henry Ford's financial choices had a significant social and economic influence in addition to revolutionizing the car business. His legacy shows how the private sector may lead to good change and serves as a model for contemporary firms.

www.ingramcontent.com/pod-product-compliance
Lightning Source LLC
Chambersburg PA
CBHW072207290526
45794CB00004B/1687